DO-DO RESCUE: FROM OVERWHELMED TO THRIVING

The Do-Be-Do-Be-Do-Be Remedy to Help You Thrive in a Crazy-Busy-World

by
Louise Lavergne

Copyright © 2019 Louise Lavergne.
Published by JoyFull Earth Productions

All rights reserved. No part of this book may be used or reproduced by any means, graphic, electronic, or mechanical, including photocopying, recording, taping or by any information storage retrieval system without the written permission of the author except in the case of brief quotations embodied in critical articles and reviews.

The names and incidents in this book have been modified to protect the privacy of individuals and to accommodate the literary flow of the book.

ISBN 978-1-951661-00-7
LCC 2019916538

The information, ideas, and suggestions in this book are not intended as a substitute for professional advice. Before following any suggestions contained in this book, you should consult your personal physician or mental health professional. Neither the author nor the publisher shall be liable or responsible for any loss or damage allegedly arising as a consequence of your use or application of any information or suggestions in this book.

Because of the dynamic nature of the Internet, any web addresses or links contained in this book may have changed since publication and may no longer be valid.

The author of this book does not dispense medical advice or prescribe the use of any technique as a form of treatment for physical, emotional, or medical problems without the advice of a physician, either directly or indirectly. The intent of the author is only to offer information of a general nature to help you in your quest for emotional and spiritual well-being. In the event you use any of the information in this book for yourself, which is your constitutional right, the author and the publisher assume no responsibility for your actions.

Any people depicted in stock imagery provided by Shutterstock are models, and such images are being used for illustrative purposes only. Some of the images in the book have been re-designed by the author.

Disclaimer:

Before doing any exercise program, please consult with your health care provider. If you are pregnant, some of the exercises in this book may not be suitable or may need modification. **It is advised that pregnant women not hold or suspend the breath in or out when doing any of these exercises.**

DEDICATION

This book is dedicated to my clients and students who have inspired me to show up, to share, and to go deeper to discover holistic techniques that are helpful and healing to the human body, mind, and spirit. You have encouraged me to create programs, classes, workshops, retreats, and more. Because of your support I was motivated to finish this book and I'm delighted to share, *Do-Do Rescue: The Do-Be-Do-Be-Do-Be Remedy* with you. More books are on the way—up next, *The Missing Peace*. Stay tuned!

Helping one person in a lifetime is a precious gift. Helping thousands of people is a privilege. Thank you, dear reader, for sitting with me while I share the beginning of my self-healing journey. I pray this book inspires you. Remember, you are the most important member of your health care team. Your power to be well depends on you becoming a mediator, creating a harmonious relationship between your body, your mind, and your spirit. You are precious. I appreciate the gift of you showing up for yourself. By making the effort to show up for inner peace, you are ultimately contributing to world peace. If we all contribute a drop, before long we will have an ocean. This book is an invitation to join me in co-creating a more "joy-full" and peaceful world.

~ Louise Lavergne

To be is to do - Socrates
To do is to be - Sartre
Do Be Do Be Do - Sinatra

~ Kurt Vonnegut

CONTENTS

ILLUSTRATIONS LIST / LIST OF PHOTOS xiii

FOREWORD xv

PREFACE xxi

ACKNOWLEDGMENTS xxvii

CHAPTER 1 - INTRODUCTION 1
    The Call to Be a Spiritual Sanitation Engineer 9

CHAPTER 2 - IDENTIFYING THE DO-DO SYNDROME 15
    If You Keep Doing and Doing, You'll End Up in Do-Do 19
    Accepting My Gift ~ Embracing My Purpose 23
    My New York Life ~ The Best and the Worst of
        Everything 28
    The Fable of Miss Independent 34
    The Do-Be-Do-Be-Do-Be Stress Test 54

**CHAPTER 3 - DO-DO RESCUE: THE DO-BE-DO-BE-DO-BE
        SOLUTION** 57
    Side Effects 58
    Your Breath, Your Belly, Your Mind 59
        Breath Affects Memory 61
    Setting Yourself Up for Success: Creating Balance 62
    The Three Keys to Success with Your BE Breaks 65
        Key #1 Positive Thinking 65
        The Positive Impact of Sound on Your Brain 66
        Affirmations You Can Use Regularly 70
        Key #2 Concentration 70
        Focus to Still Your Active Mind 72

> *Practicing Key #1 and Key #2: Sound and Mudra* 74
> *Key #3: Continuity* 75
> *Identifying Unsupportive Habits* 76
> *Choosing Supportive Habits to Commit to* 76
> Practicing the Three Keys 78
> > *Sunlight ~ Divine Light & Peace Prayer* 79

CHAPTER 4 – THE DO-DO RESCUE REMEDY 83
> The "Three Life-Saving Breaths" 83
> The Full Yogic Breath – Breathing as an Action 84
> The Power of a Conscious Breath – Breathing Like You Mean It ... 85
> Overall Benefits 86
> Strategies for Using the Full Yogic Breath Technique 86
> BE Break: "Mind-Full" Breathing to Calm Your Mind and Body 90
> BE Break: The Three Life-Saving Breaths 91
> Other Ways to Practice Your "Three Life-Saving Breaths" 93
> > BE Break: *The 4-7-8 Breath* 96
> > BE Break: *The 8-4-8-4 Breathing Ratio* 97
> The Power of Your Hands for Self-Healing 99
> Your Emotions in the Palms of Your Hands 100
> Balancing and Healing Your Whole Self, One Finger at a Time ... 102
> > BE Break: *Hands-On* 104
> > *The Thumb* 106
> > *Index Finger* 106
> > *Middle Finger* 107
> > *Ring Finger* 107
> > *Little Finger* 107
> Why Forty Days? 109
> > BE Break: Hands and Knees 113
> Accessing the Power of Your Left and Right Brain – Your Nose
> > Knows the Way 114
> > *Overall Benefits of Single or Alternate Nostril Breathing* 115
> > *Left Nostril* 116
> > *Strategies – Use this Technique:* 116
> > BE Break: *Practicing Left Nostril Breathing* 118
> > *Right Nostril* 120
> > *Strategies – Use this Technique* 120
> > BE Break: *Practicing Right Nostril Breathing* 122
> > *Alternate Nostril Breathing – Anuloma Viloma* 124
> > *Benefits* 124
> > BE Break: *Practicing Alternate Nostril Breathing* 126
> The Brain – Gut Connection 128
> Accessing the Healing Power of Your Belly 129

BE Break – *Practicing the Navel Pump* 132
The Pelvic Breath – Your Gateway to Receiving and Letting Go 134
   BE Break – *Practicing the Pelvic Breath* 138
Your Heart: The Meeting Place for Your Mind and Your Gut to
   Make Peace 140
Creating Positive Coherence 142
   BE Break – *Uniting Your Thoughts and Feelings* 144
The Healing Magic of the Cha-Cha-Cha 146
   BE Break – *The JoyFull Dynamic Movement Meditation* 150

**CHAPTER 5 - GETTING STARTED WITH YOUR DO-BE-DO-BE-
   DO-BE LIFESTYLE** 153
Three Morning Rituals to Change Your Life – One Day at a Time ... 154
Morning Ritual #1 - Loving Your Tongue ~ and Feeling Terrific 155
Morning Ritual #2 - Loving Your Gut ~ and Feeling Great 158
Morning Ritual #3 - Loving your Mind ~ Three-Minute
   Mind Shower 159
      The Practice 160
      Your Breathing 161
      Practicing the Mind Shower using Sa-Ta-Na-Ma 162

CHAPTER 6 - SWEET DREAMS ~ SWEET LIFE 165
A Good Night's Sleep Can Improve Your Day 165
Sweet Dreams: The Best Night Time Ritual to Start With 167
The Three Lists System 169
   Your Self-Care Priorities List 170
   Your Joy and Fun List 170
   Your Daily To-Do List 171

**CHAPTER 7 - GET IN THE DRIVER'S SEAT ~ BECOME THE
   HEALER OF YOUR LIFE** 173

AFTERWORD 177

List of BE Breaks
Mind-Full breathing to calm your mind and body 90
   Three Life-Saving Breaths 91
   The 4-7-8 Breath 96
   The 8-4-8-4 Breathing Ratio 97
Hands-On: Balancing and healing your whole-self one finger at a
   time. 102
   Thumb 106
   Index Finger 106

- *Middle Finger* *107*
- *Ring Finger* *107*
- *Little Finger* *107*
- Hands and Knees: When you don't know what to do 113
- Left Nostril Breathing: To relax and connect to your creativity and intuition. 116
- Right Nostril Breathing: Energize and activate your intellect. 120
- Alternate Nostril Breathing: Balancing the two hemispheres of your brain. 124
- Navel Pump: Energizing and activating the healing power of your belly. 132
- Pelvic Breath: Receiving and letting go; to harmonize your mind and belly. 134
- Uniting thoughts and feelings: Creating supportive space in your heart. 144
- The JoyFull Dynamic Meditation: To activate your joy and well-being. 150
- Mind Shower: Three minute practice to start your day with a clear mind. 159

ABOUT THE AUTHOR **183**

BIBLIOGRAPHY **185**

WORKS CITED LIST **188**

RESOURCES **191**

NOTES **192**

List of Illustrations and Photos

Illustration 1 - Inner Peace = World Peace xvii
Illustration 2 - Face the Possibilities.. xxiii
Illustration 3 - Live by Design, NOT by Default............................ 14
Illustration 4 - Stuck in Do-Do 15
Illustration 5 - Accepting Who I AM... 52
Illustration 6 - Gyan Mudra at Work 73
Illustration 7 - Hands for Kirtan Kriya 75
Illustration 8 - Prayer of Divine Light, Peace, &
    Unconditional Love 79
Illustration 9 - Affirmation Prayer... 81
Illustration 10 - BE Break - Positive Mind...................................... 86
Illustration 11 - Full Yogic Breath. 90
Illustration 12 - BE Break - Hands On 98
Illustration 13 - Emotions in Your Fingers 102
Illustration 14 - BE Break - Don't Know What to Do 105
Illustration 15 - Right and Left Brain Image 106
Illustration 16 - BE Break - Left Nostril Breath
    To Calm Your Mind... 109
Illustration 17 - Gyan Mudra 110
Illustration 18 - BE Break - Right Nostril Breath
    To Activate Your Mind 112

Illustration 19 - Surya Mudra 113
Illustration 20 - Alternate Nostril Breathing with
                 Vishnu Mudra 115
Illustration 21 - Super-Power Belt Buckle 119
Illustration 22 - BE Break - Navel Pump To Energize Yourself 120
Illustration 23 - BE Break - Pelvic Breath In and Out 123
Illustration 24 - BE Break - Thoughts and Feelings 128
Illustration 25 - BE Break - "JoyFull" Movement Meditation 132
Illustration 26 - The Pineal, Pituitary, and Thalamus Glands 139
Illustration 27 - Man Suhaavee Mudra 143
Illustration 28 - Sunlight Mind Shower 145
Illustration 29 - Get in the Driver's Seat of Your Life 155
Illustration 30 - I Choose Peace 158

FOREWORD

by Leslee Parr, PhD

We live in a culture where busyness is exalted. Overwork is admired. Constant connectivity has ratcheted up the expectations placed on us, by others and ourselves. But, chronic busyness takes a serious toll. Forty decades of stress research has shown that when stressors (negative events, chronic strains, and traumas) are measured comprehensively, their damaging impacts on physical and mental health are substantial. Being chronically busy and stressed taxes our nervous system and impairs our brain's functioning.

Stress both begins in the brain and affects the brain, as well as the rest of the body. Stressors have a major influence upon mood, our sense of well-being, behavior, and health. Brain regions such as the prefrontal cortex (higher-level thinking) and the limbic regions (responsible for emotions and memory) respond to acute and chronic stress and show changes in morphology (structure) and chemistry. Stress and other emotional responses are components of complex interactions of genetic, physiological, behavioral, and environmental factors that affect the body's ability to remain or become healthy, or to resist or overcome disease. Research shows that regulated by nervous, endocrine, and immune systems, and exerting powerful influences on other bodily systems and key health-relevant behaviors, stress and emotion have important implications for the initiation or progression of cancer, cardiovascular disease, and other illnesses.

Perhaps more profoundly, recent research shows that stress actually changes the composition and the functioning of our DNA. A range of recent studies have identified structural changes at specific genes, and throughout the genome, in association with multiple psychosocial stressors in a process called 'epigenetic DNA methylation.' As difficult as it may be to comprehend, these changes can actually be passed down to our offspring and on to future generations.

As a genetics scientist and Professor, it is easier for me to summon those words than it has been to take action to mitigate or curtail the siren call of high expectation in my own life.

Knowing full well that life within the academic pressure-cooker was busy methylating my DNA and wreaking havoc on my immune system, I could not bring myself to sacrifice productivity for peace nor success for sleep. I was sure that if I could just make that next grant deadline, and get my next graduate student graduated, THEN I would have time to restart my formerly healthy lifestyle.

This all began to change when I joined Louise Lavergne's JoyFull Yoga practice. As Louise pointed out to me, taking the time to care for myself *within* the context of my life's obligations was the first and most vital step. Louise's guidance in class was masterful and fun. It was easy to follow her cueing on exercises which spanned the range from calming to invigorating, challenging to peace-generating. Louise's classes pack in an exhilarating combination of yoga, dance, voice and movement meditation, as well as sound healing. Surprisingly, I found myself smiling, chanting, singing, dancing, and occasionally even laughing.

Having been a teacher and a Professor for over forty years, as well as a master mentor to young PhDs for the National Institute of Health, I immediately recognized Louise as a truly gifted and masterful teacher. Research on effective teaching demonstrates that students learn best and retain knowledge and technique most effectively when their learning environment is stress-free and fun. Whether studied or intuitive, Louise creates just such an environment in her classes.

I left Louise's JoyFull studio feeling somehow lighter, maybe even brighter. I left with a sense of empowerment and a smile on my face. Two years later, firmly committed to a journey of self-healing, I still leave her studio refreshed, lightened, more hopeful, and optimistic about my day, my life and, more profoundly, about all life on this earth we inhabit. The demands on my time and the external stressors that surround me have not lessened, but I truly believe that incorporating Louise's techniques and exercises have helped me to feel more grounded and have allowed me to take better control of how I experience and react to life and therefore how I influence the lives of those around me more positively. As Louise says, *"You may not always be able to control external circumstances, but you always have a choice regarding how you meet any situation."*

I was one of the lucky few. Chance, fortune, and proximity led me to Louise's JoyFull Yoga studio. When Louise gave me the privilege of reading an advanced copy of this, her second book, *Do-Do Rescue: The Do-Be-Do-Be-Do-Be Remedy to Help You Thrive in a Crazy-Busy World*, I wondered if she could capture in print the clarity and spirit of her live classroom. I am happy to report that she has done that brilliantly. Her gentle, wise voice speaks clearly from these pages. Her light-hearted take on her life's journey helps the reader to keep life's dramas in perspective. More than all of that, this book provides the reader with an in-hand, always-accessible reference.

Woven throughout the techniques and practices that Louise gives to you on these pages, you will find Louise's captivating personal story. Through her life adventures, Louise shows us that although she often seems a 'goddess,' she is in fact a real person who lived through and learned from very real problems. You will learn that it was real life, with more than the usual hard knocks, which paved Louise's own journey to wisdom. When Louise speaks to you on these pages, it becomes clear that she doesn't have unrealistic expectations for you, she knows all about the do-do side of life and the challenges of transitioning to a Do-Be-Do-Be-Do-Be way of living.

With this book in your hand, you now have an easy-to-follow guide, a 'toolkit' packed with clear directions, effective techniques, and simple approaches for establishing your foundational practice. Here, Louise provides you with small steps easily incorporated into a busy day. She gives you helpful suggestions for transitioning into and then maintaining the Do-Be-Do-Be-Do-Be lifestyle. This book is a hard-copy catalogue of the techniques, practices, and even a few healthful recipes that Louise has developed over decades of her own study and practice. You will be able to turn to these pages again and again for reference and motivation.

The combined results of four decades of research has made clear to scientists and health care practitioners like myself that the impacts of stressors on health and well-being are reduced when persons achieve high levels of mastery and self-esteem. With this book, you own an easy-to- follow roadmap to mastery, one that will help you to reclaim your authentic power and improve your confidence and well-being in each moment of your life. With this guide, you too can create a harmonious relationship between your body, your mind, your spirit, your life, and the lives of those around you.

Leslee Parr, PhD

"If you want to live in a peaceful world, start by creating peace in your own body and in your own life."

~ Louise Lavergne

PREFACE

If you have just opened this book, it's likely that you have an interest in what you can do to feel better. Most likely, you want more than just a medical protocol to achieve it. I often hear, "I want to do your program because I believe in 'mind over matter.' " For example, a woman named Judy came up to me after one of my workshops, enthusiastic about incorporating Mind/Body practices into her recovery from breast cancer. "I believe in mind over matter," she said with stern determination, as if she was entering a cage to tame her lion-mind. Now, there is some truth in that concept—in that "if you don't mind, it doesn't matter." But this belief can set you up for a tug-of-war between your mind and the reality you are in.

This book and my programs are not so much about mind over matter. Rather, I suggest that instead of fighting the mind (and making it the enemy) that you go into partnership with your mind, your body, and your spirit. Thinking of "your happy place" while your ship is sinking isn't going to save you. It may distract you and help you forget about it for a little while, but the fact is that if there is a leak in your vessel, you have to take time to repair it.

Vacillating between frantic moments of bailing water and pausing to forget about it is exhausting. The fear of your boat going down never really goes away. I'm suggesting that you take action, moment by moment, that supports you in navigating and repairing your lifeboat while also supporting your intention to be well. I'm inviting you to be motivated by love instead of fear, and to spend time on your most precious resource: you. Put down your bucket and stop bailing. Trying to fix yourself and other people is tiring. Instead, let's take care of the energy leaks in your body and in your life. I'm inviting you to swim to shore so you can catch your breath and begin your restoration process. From there, I will guide you to reclaim a life that supports you, your success, *and* your health.

When it comes to taking a Mind, Body, Spirit approach to wellness, there's often an underlying implication that your mind (your intellectual gift) is a bad thing and that the spiritual part of you is "better" or more important. The fact is that every part of you is important. The process of creating a mind-spirit partnership instills in you a greater sense of respect, both for your intellectual gift (that wants to understand) and your intuitive gift (that wants to feel).

When the mind and the spirit work together, you have an enhanced ability to discern and make supportive choices moment by moment. I want to help you understand the possibilities so your mind can relax, which in turn will help your whole body relax. This is a way for you to experience the Mind-Body-Spirit approach to wellness. This partnership will support you on your holistic healing journey. (According to *dictionary.com*, "holistic" means "incorporating…the idea that the whole is more than merely the sum of its parts, in theory or practice.")

Your mind and your thoughts play a big part in your success. If you think something isn't going to work, you're right. It won't. But if you can practice meeting what is unfolding in your life without judgment and keep an open mind by being curious about what is possible, then amazing things can open up for you. Spiritual experiences can give you a reprieve from a challenging reality. It can also become an escape rather than a source of healing. Positive thoughts that you "know" aren't true, can distract your mind momentarily. When reality hits you (your body is not well, you don't have the money to pay your bills, or your boss didn't approve your vacation, or fill in the blank) everything that is not working in your life hits you like a bucket of ice water, leaving you feeling more discordant and resentful. Choosing to redirect your mind towards compassion and presence, as well as slowing down your body moment by moment within your reality, creates transitional steps towards transformation. This nurtures an honest and harmonious partnership between mind and matter, spirit, and body that will allow you to have it all. It allows you to sustain a life that is both successful and balanced at the same time. When you stop trying or wishing for things to be different or for you to be something other than who you are, you will find that you have more energy. It's so much easier to be yourself. Trying to keep up with being something you're not is exhausting.

It's equally draining to not be honest about what you are feeling in the moment. Saying, "It's all good" in times of crisis keeps you in a lie. If you are affirming to yourself and to the Universe that a challenging situation *is* "all good," then why change anything? Be clear about what you define as "good." Another way you can get stuck in a lie can come from well-meaning caregivers telling you, "It's okay to not be okay." Is it really? Can you tell me honestly that you are happy about your current challenges? It's not okay that you are suffering *and* it's not okay to beat yourself up about it. I am deeply sorry for your pain. I want to remind you that it's more important that you meet your reality with honesty *and* compassion: *"I'm not okay right at this moment ... but I meet myself in this moment* with compassion. I'm willing to take responsibility and do my part to heal and move toward a solution to feel better."

When things are challenging, it's okay to acknowledge that it sucks. It's equally important that you take steps toward feeling better. Unfortunately, it's sometimes easier to ignore or numb the call of pain. When you are stuck in mad you can't get glad.

"I just don't know what to do to help myself."

If you feel like you don't know what to do to help yourself, it is my wish that you discover reliable, actionable solutions that will move you toward healing and restoring your whole self and your life. It's time to stop the tug-of-war between mind and spirit. In this book, I introduce you to ideas and techniques that will help you to create a partnership that respects your intellect *and* your spirit. Whatever is going on in your life right now matters—but it's not the only thing that matters.

If you think that living a balanced life needs to wait until your life is less busy, or if you think you have to choose between success and a balanced life ... you don't! I have written this book to share with you a viable way for you to have it all: a busy, prosperous, healthy, balanced life that gives you (and the people around you) JOY.

If you want to be happy and live a sustainable, abundant, healthy, and joyful life, this book is a great place for you to start. I hope you enjoy it.

~ Louise Lavergne

Face the unknown with curiosity and
BE open up to possibilites
that support you
and your Higher good.

Asking yourself deeper questions opens up new ways of being in the world. It brings in a breath of fresh air. It makes life more joyful. The real trick to life is not to be in the know, but to be in the mystery.

~ Fred Alan Wolf, Physicist

ACKNOWLEDGMENTS

I want to thank my mother for giving me life and supporting me along my journey—without understanding what and why I did what I did most of the time. She is the one who has made it possible for me to publish this book, as well as her loving husband, my step-dad, Claude. (My mom remarried at age 78.) I love you and so appreciate you both. Merci, Maman, for showing up and being there for my kids when I needed you. Merci, Maman, for inspiring in me the faith of a loving God. Merci, Maman, for teaching me the power of prayer in dark times. Merci, Maman, for reminding me to call in the power of Holy Spirit when I forgot to and was afraid of the unknown. Thank for your relentless prayers for my family and me. Nobody can pray like my Mama prays. This book is here to prove it.

I want to thank my children for giving me the anchors to be here and rise above the challenges. My dear son, you have pushed me to go beyond what I could imagine possible. You continue to inspire me to practice being. I hope you know how much I love you. My dear daughter, thank you for your love and support. Thank you for making it possible for me to do what I do and be who I am. It's not always easy for you to share your mom. I am so grateful for your loving presence and support in my life.

Thank you to my soul sisters along the way. Lise-Anne je t'aime toujours. Joanie, you are now and always my rock and my sister in every way. Thank you, Elizabeth, for always being there for me, especially at the birth of my son. Wendy, thank you for all your support and for all the wonderful, nurturing, and memorable moments in the country. Alice, thank you for your loving presence in my life and for your support through my intense New York Do-Do period and beyond. Tracey and Suzanne, I love you and so appreciate you both in my life. Thank you, Tracey, for the wonderful pictures of me in this book that capture my inner spirit and Suzanne for helping us make it happen, inside and out. Thayne, thank you for your care and amazing talent in creating the cover of the book.

Thank you, Leslee, for writing the Foreword to this book. It makes me so happy to know that this book has helped you. Your passion for this work inspires me, and your contribution and support with this book mean so much to me. Gesine, your thoughtful insights and feedback have been invaluable.

Tammey, thank you for writing the Afterword and giving us an inspiring ending. It has been one of my great joys to see you continue to blossom through the years. Your courage inspires me.

I want to thank my editor, Michael Ireland, whose support and insights have helped to make this book shine. Thank you for your encouragement along the way to keep going. It was such a gift to work with a soul-sister. And of course, thank you to my PRESStinely team, Kristen, Maira and Dawn, you are awesome. Thank you for your creativity and support in helping me make this book a reality.

To my partner and adopted family member, Michael, thank you is not enough. You are a "God bless" in our lives. Thank you for being there for me and my family. Thank you for showing up for me over and over, always with unconditional love and integrity. Thank you for loving me for who I am and for listening to every idea, inspiration, and challenge. Mostly, thank you for giving me the gift of sharing a life of true unconditional love, relentless peace, and adventure.

I want to thank all my teachers and the thought leaders who have inspired me, especially Paramahansa Yogananda, Swami Vishnudevananda, Yogi Bhajan, Dr. Joseph Michael Levry, and Mantak Chia. I want to thank Dr. Robin Miller and Dr. Prachi Garodia for your collaboration and sharing your wisdom with me.

To all my Foundation 4 Your L.I.F.E. clients and JoyFull Yoga students, I am so grateful for your support and inspiration.

I have an amazing behind-the-scenes team that makes it all possible for me. Divine Spirit, all the angels, archangels, and ancient sages that work through me, I feel blessed and grateful for your presence in my work and in my life. It does take a village.

With Love and Light,
Namaste,
Louise

CHAPTER 1
INTRODUCTION

It's easy to get pulled into the demands of our fast-paced world. From the moment you wake up each morning, your mind is standing by, waiting for your cue to get going on something. So many things pull at you to get your attention. You get sucked into the emails, the texts. Next thing you know you're pouring coffee but you forgot the cup. You may buy into the belief that the responsible thing to do is to respond to all external demands. The habit of looking at your phone within the first fifteen minutes of your day, for example, can cost you the ability to discern what is important to *you*. You might have forgotten that you have a choice about what you give your energy to.

> **"You have a choice about what you give your energy to."**

Do you get swept up in trying to keep up with external demands—like your job or other people's needs? Does everything around you feel more important than your own personal needs? Are you surrounded by drama in your life, yours and other people's? If you feel that fear and worry are the reasons for your actions and decisions; if you feel like you run from crisis to crisis or from one chaotic event to another, and you find yourself feeling like you don't have enough energy and time in your day, this book was written for you. *Do-Do Rescue* offers you a simple, effective map to guide you to take back control of your day—and ultimately, your life.

In Chapter 2, I share some of my personal story and explain how, in my younger years, I experienced the disempowering impact of not effectively managing the daily stress of my busy lifestyle as a new mother. I share how being creative with my time and obligations allowed me to include spiritual awareness, yoga, and meditation in my every day, crazy-busy reality. Self-care made all the difference—and I was able to reclaim my inner power! I reveal the turning point in my self-healing journey, where I embraced the importance of healing myself before I could be of service to others. Finally, I show you how those pursuits led me to the creation of the Do-Be-Do-Be-Do-Be Remedy, and how using the remedy rescued me from the trap of overdoing—or what I call, "Do-Do."

In Chapter 3, I address how you can take care of your whole self, by practicing effective, supportive techniques I call BE Breaks. You'll learn how to connect into your whole being ... from your Belly to your Mind to your Heart. In Chapter 4, you'll find a series of life-changing BE Break exercises, followed by some helpful action items and habits to support you in sustaining and enhancing the benefits of a Do-Be-Do-Be-Do-Be lifestyle. In Chapter 5, I share three of my most life-changing morning habits to start your day. The information in Chapter 6 is to help you with the end of your day.

Throughout this book, I offer you easy but powerful suggestions that can be a crucial part of breaking out of your unsupportive habits and building confidence and success with your more supportive ones. I have included some Notes Pages in the back of the book so that as you move through the book, you can write down any ideas you want to begin to include in your day. I suggest you also dedicate a lined notebook (or two!) to your Do-Be-Do-Be-Do-Be journey, so you can document your progress with each of the practices you want to incorporate into your daily lifestyle. My clients and students have shared with me the activities we have done together that have made the biggest differences in their lives. I have included some of these in this book. I have also included some of my own personal stories as examples of how I moved from a busy Do-Do life into a Do-Be-Do-Be-Do-Be lifestyle. (Please note that the names and incidents in this book have been modified to protect the privacy of individuals and to accommodate the literary flow of the book.)

I know from experience that when you are feeling constantly out of balance, pushing to keep up with only your external demands, it's a lot like trying to do life standing on one leg. With this book, I'm here to extend a hand, to remind you to stop the habits that lead you into a state of overwhelm. You and only you can stop the insanity of "...doing the same thing over and over again, but expecting different results," as Einstein is credited with saying. We're living in a time when we have the opportunity to upgrade our quality of life. I'm excited to share with you how you can do that *right now*. It's so much easier to navigate the events of your day when you take time to get both of your feet on the ground. As you learn to practice my "Do-Be-Do-Be-Do-Be" rhythm throughout your day, you'll begin to create a healing relationship with your body. You'll reclaim your authentic power and improve your confidence and well-being, moment by moment.

An unattended mind doesn't discriminate. It has a simple rule: pay attention to whatever is loudest. You know you "should" take better care of yourself. With good intentions, you want to, but there seems to be no responsible way and no time to do it. Taking care of external demands first is an easy habit to fall into because outside stressors are the most obvious. If you don't take out the trash, for example, sooner or later, you see and smell the consequences. Did you know that the same goes for your internal needs? When you don't clear out your mental trash—worry, fear, negative self-talk, your emotional state—it starts to stink. The negative impact may not be noticeable immediately. But a negative thought over time can be the seed that grows into back pain, inflammation, and other aches and pains. At first, it's easy to ignore the connection. You might opt for a quick fix—a pill, alcohol, or other socially acceptable numbing substances—that can keep you going with what you have to DO.

Currently, many people seem obsessed, trying to keep up with everything that demands our attention. Your phone beeps … there's a new text, an email, a Facebook post. You don't want to miss a thing. It feels impossible to cut anyone or anything off the to-do list until your body—or your life—falls apart and the quick fixes stop working. Holding on to a negative thought or resentment is a lot like holding a pencil. It doesn't seem like a big deal at first. What harm can a little pencil (or a little thought) have? But try holding a pencil for an hour, two, three … the pain can become debilitating. The same goes for a negative thought. American psychiatrist, Dr. Aaron T. Beck, known as the father of cognitive therapy, conducted studies in the 1960's on the impact negative thoughts have on our health and behavior. Holding on to negative thoughts about yourself, the world, or the future has a profound impact on how you feel, emotionally and physically. Happily, there is a cure: STOP IT! Put the pencil down. In this book, I'm going to show you how you can take out the mental trash—even when you think you don't have time.

> *"The greatest discovery of my generation is that human beings can change the quality of their lives by changing the attitudes of their minds."*
> ~ **William James**

It all comes down to a simple fact: *Living life at warp speed is exhausting.* When you ignore the signals that you and your life are out of balance, when you keep on doing and doing, you end up in what I call the "Do-Do syndrome." When you are stuck in Doing and Doing, sooner or later your health—and your life—ends up in deep Doo-Doo.

Why is everything (and everybody else's need) more important than your own well-being? I know first-hand that putting others first is a hard habit to break.

For me, putting other's needs first started in childhood. When I was nine years old, my parents were going through a tumultuous divorce. My mother's health was affected by the stress and strain to the point where she could no longer take care of us. My two brothers and I ended up living with my dad. Being the only girl and the middle child, my father crowned me "lady of the house." I didn't understand what that meant until I wanted to go to my gymnastics practice. My dad pointed to the laundry and other household chores that needed to be done. How could I be so selfish? My father shamed me for wanting to do something for myself before taking care of everyone else's needs. I had been selected to try out to qualify for an upcoming competition. My first one. Not going to practice that day meant I was missing my chance.

Saying no to my dad was never an option for me. I accepted that what I wanted was not as important as what needed to be done. I was driven by the fear of the consequences of making Daddy mad. I gave into the tasks, feeling sorry for myself. My father was used to getting his way. I was taught to not rock the boat, to do "what Daddy says." I was also motivated by the notion that doing what makes people happy would grant me approval and acceptance. I was driven by my need to create peace in the house. As many of us learn as children, I thought "if I am good and I do what I can to make the adults happy," that would assure peace in the house, and we would be safe and loved.

This is where one of my shame stories began. These stories shape our belief system; I call them "shame seeds." This particular one is about believing that tending to my needs before others' needs was selfish and bad. A good person tends to other people's needs only. I wanted to be a good girl. Doing for others was also an effective way for me to earn my worth in any situation. If I was a guest in someone's home, for example, I would quickly jump to help with cooking or the cleaning up to earn my worth as a guest. It always got me praise from the adults.

Do you ever feel guilty about doing something that is "just" for your own well-being? Do you feel guilty and feel that you have to justify taking time for yourself (like when you are sick)? For many of us, this habit is fueled by the need for external approval and validation. Do you believe that what you do is tied to being loved and accepted? Do you qualify self-care time as luxurious or frivolous and not valuable? That feeling is fueled by the illusion that you can trump your self-worth by improving your net worth. This debilitating conditioning is also a common seed of low self-esteem and low self-worth. It was for me. I learned the hard way that I don't need my body to break down to justify taking care of myself. You don't either. It was a long road on the self-healing journey that inspired many of my current programs. I feel so grateful to be able to share some of this with you in this book.

You are precious. Please know that honoring the gift of you is one of your gifts to the world. When you take care of yourself, it opens the door for others to do the same. You inspire others to also practice self-care. Can you imagine a world in which everyone shows up feeling their best?

Remember the Golden Rule from Jesus's Sermon on the Mount: *Do to others as you would have them do to you.* Be part of the chain reaction. Give yourself as much respect as you give others and others will respect you. Self-respect includes being respectful of your energy. What are you craving the most from other people? Love? Self-care is self-love. You want to be heard? Start listening more attentively to others *and* to yourself and to your body. You want flowers? Buy yourself flowers. A good way to catch yourself if you are respecting your energy is to write a to-do list. Look at your list. Is it only about taking care of others? Does your to-do list make you feel defeated at the end of the day? Would you expect anyone else to get this much done in a day?

It's okay to be busy. By shifting to a "Do-Be-Do-Be-Do-Be" list, you will be able to get things done and be able to end your day feeling inspired and energized. It comes down to common sense ... taking care of yourself *within* all of your obligations, while doing what needs your attention. As long as you just keep trying to keep up and keep juggling everything, you will never feel balanced. There is no end to the things that need doing. Have you ever noticed that the more you do, the more there is to do? The extra time you are waiting for—so you can take care of your own needs—never magically appears. As I said earlier, when you are stuck in "Do-Do mode," sooner or later, your health and your life end up in deep Doo-Doo. You are heading for burnout—or worse.

With the Do-Be-Do-Be-Do-Be system, balance *can* coexist with a busy lifestyle.

In this book, I share with you my solution to shift your day strategically—out of "Do-Do mode" and into a "Do-Be-Do-Be-Do-Be" rhythm—so you can end your day feeling more inspired and energized. Imagine yourself smiling at the end of your day. You don't need to wait for that long-anticipated vacation or for when you have more time (ha, never!). When you consistently balance your "doing" with specific "BE Breaks" on a day-to-day basis, you can still be a busy person and create a successful, healthy, prosperous, balanced, and joy-full life.

The Do-Be-Do-Be-Do-Be rhythm is an efficient and sustainable way for you to keep up with your external and internal needs while meeting the demands of your day. I'm going to make it easy for you to start creating more balance in your body and in your life, from where you are right now. I know from my own experience (and from the experiences of my high-achieving clients) that balance *can* coexist with a busy lifestyle. My Do-Be-Do-Be-Do-Be system allows you to flow with all that supports what is important to you and your LIFE:

Love, Inspiration, Freedom, and Empowerment.

Get ready to step out of the Do-Do syndrome and claim the driver's seat of your life!

THE CALL TO BE A SPIRITUAL SANITATION ENGINEER

During that challenging time of living with my father, I had a mystical experience that propelled me forward on my spiritual quest for peace and balance. As a child, my life experience was often about coping with being afraid all the time. I write about this in greater depth in my upcoming book, *The Missing Peace*. I want to share a story from the book with you because it was this one particular episode that impelled me to help myself and others to restore inner peace and balance. It was my first lesson on the long path to accepting my life's mission to help others as a "Spiritual Sanitation Engineer."

I was alone in the living room with my father. He was in complete overwhelm and was letting me know that he was looking into foster care for us kids. He got furious when I asked that I not be separated from my little brother. I had stepped on a land mine. His anger exploded as he grabbed me. I was terrified. The doorbell rang—my uncle Bob had come by to say hi. I was left alone, upstairs, everyone else was downstairs in the family room. I was crying, feeling helpless, scared. What was going to happen to us? The crying turned into an anxiety attack, I was struggling to catch my breath. I became even more terrified. My arms felt numb, I didn't know what to do. I fell down on the couch. I stopped breathing. The next thing I knew, I felt the fear melt, like ice in fire, and found myself in the most exquisite place. It felt like being home, but in a way I had never experienced "home." It looked like a crystal planet to me, full of light, peaceful.

In that amazing place, I felt a depth of love that is not possible to describe with words. I saw people that, though I had never seen them before, felt familiar. For the first time in my short life, I felt like I belonged, I felt embraced and loved.

All the fear left my body as they reassured me that all would be well, that I was not alone. They were looking out for me. All the stress I didn't know I was holding in my little body went away. I felt peaceful in a way I didn't know was possible. Then, a beautiful lady said in a loving voice that I needed to go back. It wasn't my time to come home yet. I remember not wanting to go back to the drama of my life. But I thought about my little brother and somehow, I understood. They reassured me that when I felt things getting dark, all I needed to do was to connect to God's Light. I needed to breathe in Light and breathe out Light. I knew, deep in my heart, what they meant. The lady said I needed to go back so I could help others remember that the Light is always there.

I came out of this experience changed forever. It was many years later that I realized this was a Near Death Experience (NDE). What I remember most is the deep peace and profound love I felt. It thrust me into a lifelong quest to learn everything I could about how to connect with this kind of Light. It was beyond the peace I felt in my times of prayer. It included the physical experience of peace. I knew it had something to do with my breathing.

When I "woke up," in my child's mind, I didn't understand the full message the spirit people had given me. Years later, I understood what they meant. I was here to help others "find their inner Light switch." I felt a lingering peace in my heart that day. It gave me a strength that continued to help me navigate my life with a grateful heart. I understood somehow that all the challenges in my life were giving me a strength and compassion that would help me to help others and myself get through the bumpy parts of life. I could see that my father was suffering. All I could feel was compassion for him.

My mother was getting better and she arranged for us to have a visiting day with her. I saw that she was well enough for me to tell her about my father's idea of putting us in foster care. I'm not sure how it all happened, but she talked with my dad and a few weeks later they got back together. Two years later, they were divorced for good. My mom stopped listening to her lawyer. She gave up the fight to keep the house and her struggle for child support. We left everything behind except our clothes and moved away to begin our new life.

I didn't see my father again until my early twenties. But I'd learned from my dad's behavior how stress and overwhelm can turn a loving person into a monster. And I saw how it made my mom so sick that she would leave us. Interestingly, in the last year of my dad's life, over thirty years later, she was by his side taking care of him. I learned a lot about the healing power of forgiveness from my mother.

As human beings, a big part of our journey is remembering who we truly are. When you are stressed out, it is easy to become the worst version of yourself because stress makes you forget who you really are. Stress and fear activate your pseudo-powers that bully you into doing what you know is "good" for you—or else! But it's like going on a crash diet; you only get short-term results. You lose weight only to gain it all back (or more) within a short time period. Your bully powers only give you the illusion of power. Anything you do that is good for you, when fueled by fear-based motives, will not give you long-term results. But when you are balanced, stress and fear are less likely to be the drivers—*you* will be in the driver's seat. From there, you can access your authentic power.

By remembering to take charge of your breathing, you can begin to regain your power and balance. So, I started to learn how my breathing could impact my physical state of being. By slowing down my breathing, I could access a feeling of peace similar to what I had felt on the crystal planet. I could access a deeper part of myself. I knew nothing about meditation but I knew about talking to God through prayer. I would ask for guidance from my peaceful heart. I was "taught" how to create a wonderful experience in my physical body and my heart that I called visiting "my home-light."

In my college years and into my twenties, I was an aspiring actor. I also wanted to learn everything I could about metaphysics, psychology, nutrition, and spirituality. After I graduated from a reputable theatre program, I quickly became a working actor. I soon left my home town of Montreal and relocated to Toronto where an agent wanted to represent me. This was early in my career—it felt like a big deal and worth the move. I was a French-Canadian redhead (still am) so it was hard to get parts in just French-Canadian casting calls. But thanks to my father's business sense, I'd gone to an English high school and college. In Toronto I was getting acting work in both French and English. My acting work began to flourish with TV commercials and bilingual training videos, and before long it afforded me the time and money I needed to learn all I could about my spiritual gifts.

I have had the great privilege of learning from amazing teachers who showed up along the path on my journey toward wholeness, health, and healing. All of the wisdom of many ancient masters is now part of the practice of integrative medicine. Yoga and color therapy, Reiki and Chi Gong, astral travel and herbs, Ayurveda (an ancient Indian science of Mind-Body wellness) and nutrition … all have been part of my self-healing journey. The integration of all that I have learned on my path, from overcoming my struggles to creating balance, is what I share with you here. The Do-Be-Do-Be-Do-Be way of life is an invitation for you to embark on your own self-healing journey to create balance from a place that respects and honors who you are and where you are right now.

Balance is what makes feeling good possible. It starts with you being in a harmonious partnership with your body and your mind and your spiritual nature. You (and only you) can create a supportive environment for your body and your mind to be able to do their job efficiently. By setting the stage on the inside, you can accomplish what you want to do and become who you want to be. It's not one *or* the other. Imagine working for someone who is always screaming at you, expressing discontent and frustration. Would you be able to do a good job in that kind of stressful environment? Think about how you feel when someone takes time to listen to you ... without judging you. Your body deserves nothing less. Your body is designed to be well but it needs your participation. It craves love the way a baby does. Each ache you feel in your body is saying, "Please love me." It's more common for us to get mad at a body part like an aching knee or sore shoulder as we struggle with the inconvenience of not being able to do what we used to be able to do prior to the debilitating pain showing up. In this book, you will learn to create a supportive, loving working environment for your body. You will learn to activate your body's and your mind's superpowers at any time you need them, through (among other things) taking balancing breaks I call "BE Breaks." When you feel balanced, it's much easier to remember where your inner Light switch is when things get dark and challenging. You can remember that eating the whole cake is not a good idea. *With your inner Light on, you can make supportive choices and decisions that move you forward toward your health and personal goals and aspirations.* By reading this book, you will know what kind of BE Break to take any time you need more energy, what kind of BE Break to take for clarity, and what kind of BE Break will help relax you for a good night's sleep. Each type of Break is a practice, which means you don't have to be perfect. Each time you practice a BE Break, it will help you lower your stress levels so you can manage stress throughout your day. This is how you can avoid the pitfalls of overwhelm and burn out.

I have designed each BE Break to help you meet the demands of your busy world without compromising your health and happiness. BE Breaks are like signs along the road, guiding you toward living your life by design, not by default. When you put BE Breaks into practice, you'll start to recognize when fear and overwhelm are in the driver's seat, leading you downhill in the wrong direction—you'll have the power to stop before you get lost, and get back on track. In Chapter 4, the list of BE Breaks offers you strategies and suggestions on which BE Break to use for specific times or circumstances. But first, let's start by understanding how easy it is to let fear and drama take the wheel in the first place.

CHAPTER 2
IDENTIFYING THE
DO-DO SYNDROME

The Do-Do syndrome can start with good intentions that sweep you onto a busy super-highway as you try to make your life better by getting everything done. Stress keeps happiness at arm's length. It makes you feel like "anytime now" you'll be able to pull into the fast lane and put the pedal to the metal ... so you keep going. It can start with something as simple as an unrealistic to-do list that becomes a source of exhaustion, making it hard for you to find the off-ramp.

You may think of self-care as a luxury. But self-care and balance have to be part of a sustainable, healthy, and happy life. "I want to take care of myself, but right now I just have too much on my plate." Having "too much on your plate" is habit. That is exactly when you need the extra boost. Can you imagine putting gas in your car only when you have time?

If you don't make the time, the car stops. Self-care is like refueling your inner engine. For your body to survive and thrive, self-care is as important as breathing. Yet I often hear my clients say, "But I just don't have the time." Do *you* think of self-care as frivolous or selfish? Of course, it's easy to ignore its importance since the immediate, external consequences are not as obvious as they are with your car.

Self-care is not rewarded socially. You won't win awards for taking "the best care of yourself." Your boss is not likely to give you a raise for not burning out. As noted, the habit of making everything but your self-care important is hard to break, but it is a crucial part of solving any problems in your life right now. Over time, getting stuck in Do-Do mode can cause you to lose what you are working so hard to accomplish. It can cost you your life. Imagine, for example, having a certain amount of money to sustain your life. If you keep spending and you don't invest or take time to generate more money, you *will* run out. The same is true for your body's energy and well-being. BE Breaks are a chance for you to invest in—and harvest—your inner resources, so your body performs at its best and you can thrive and *live your optimal life.*

Do you believe that if you stop doing, you will lose everything? There is a residual "caveman brain" belief that if you stop running, the dinosaur is going to get you. That's why we have a natural, built-in resistance to creating more balance. Survival mode tells you to run and not look back. It fuels an underlying fear that balance can't coexist with your busy, high-achieving lifestyle. You have an innate opposition to a stress-free life because it goes against your primal survival instincts to stay alive. Your deep inner wisdom knows that there's no such thing as a stress-free life … until you are dead and gone. The fear of balance is tied to the fear of dying.

Funny thing about a stressed-out life, you keep running away and toward the same thing. Ever watched a dog chasing its tail? That's a Do-Do life predicament.

People often say to me: "If only I had a stress-free life. Then I'd have a balanced life."

It's important to understand that a balanced life isn't achieved once you have a stress-free life. Stress in and of itself is not bad. The fact is, life by its nature is stressful; stress is part of the body's natural survival mechanism. Our bodies create two hormones: adrenaline and cortisol, to give us an extra boost and motivation to meet the demands of stressful life situations. Stressful events can be happy (like getting your dream job) or sad (like losing your job). Both events cause elevated levels of hormones. When your body produces too much stress hormone, too often and for too long, your body can break down and create a wide range of health problems.

According to reports by the National Institute for Occupational Safety and Health, stress is linked to ninety percent of illness and disease. Personally, I think it's more like ninety-nine percent because every problem I've ever met in my life (and in my clients' lives) has had a stress component. That's insane ... and it's indicative of the state of our world. Stress affects your performance. It reduces your ability to be productive. It can become so debilitating that it prevents you from meeting the demands of your job, your relationships, and your health. Even if you're the most qualified and experienced person in your world, if stress creeps in, it becomes challenging to sustain your success.

The repercussions of continuous stress in your body often trickle out into your personal and professional life. Relationships are altered when stress is present. Stress affects how you interact with your co-workers, partners, children, friends, and family members. You can get caught up in a cyclical pattern of lashing out due to stress, and then feeling horrible about your behavior, which causes even more stress. And, when you get stuck in Do-Do syndrome, you can't see the hole you are digging. Unresolved stress leads to overwhelm.

When you invest all of your time in taking care of external demands, your fuel gauge drops and, since your car can't run on empty, it stalls. As noted earlier, what would happen if you never made time to refuel your vehicle? You'd run out of gas on the freeway and cause a traffic jam. That kind of stress can deplete your ability to think clearly, so you can't even think of a simple solution like calling a tow truck. Instead, you try to push the car. No wonder you feel exhausted during crazy periods of high stress.

The Do-Do syndrome pulls you into an endless marathon that leaves you feeling overwhelmed, which leads to even higher levels of stress and anxiety. Yet somehow, overwhelm is justified as a necessary evil of a modern lifestyle. Being overwhelmed has become an acceptable price to pay for success. But, in the midst of overwhelm, the quest for balance pulls at you. It feeds your feelings of guilt. You know you have to get around to it.

If you are overwhelmed, you may accept the habitual feeling of dread when you wake up each morning. To avoid feeling that way, you just jump right back into another "Do-Do" day. Do you remember the last time you felt really good during a non-vacation day? Do you ever catch yourself in a daydream about the weekend or taking time off? Do you feel like there's nothing you can do about whatever is challenging you right now? Do you wish things were different? Do you ever feel powerless, stuck, exhausted?

Overwhelm happens slowly over time. It makes you feel like you don't have a choice. You might feel helpless and disconnected from your needs but as long as you stay busy, you can avoid thinking about it and ignore your feelings. The fog of depression can seep in. That's when you can lose sight of what really matters, which makes it difficult to make supportive choices about anything and everything: food, relationships, health, money, etc. It's pretty easy, for the most part, to fill all your pauses with distractions. When a pause sneaks in, there is always ... Facebook or Instagram (or whatever the latest one is at the time you read this book!). You look at all those happy people and wonder, "Why can't I do it? I'd better try harder or I'll lose everything." You compare yourself. You judge yourself. Now you feel even worse about yourself and your life. Being stuck in Do-Do syndrome stinks! But there is another choice you can make. Yes, there's hope!

IF YOU KEEP DOING AND DOING, YOU'LL END UP IN DO-DO

I didn't know I was in overwhelm or in Do-Do. It happened over time. I dug myself into a big hole, one Do-Do day at a time. To avoid digging your own Do-Do hole, it's important to understand the inner story that's pulling you out of balance and putting you on the road to Do-Do overwhelm.

People like to blame external circumstances for the stress and overwhelm they experience. You may not always be able to control external circumstances, but you always have a choice regarding how you meet any situation. Taking action that supports you in any given moment will help you feel more grounded and let you take control of your life experience. When your day (and your life) becomes about trying to keep up with external demands and you are always "shoulding" on yourself ... "*I should do this or I should do that*" ... you are doing the walk of shame and that will mostly likely lead you into Do-Do mode. Where there is a "should," there is a seed of an old story of shame or a fear-based motive that doesn't serve you anymore.

Start by giving yourself permission right now to let "should" go. Reframe every "should" with a choice. "I choose to take a moment to breathe." Or, "I'm choosing *not* to eat the whole cake because I care about myself and my well-being." Let go of perfection and make space in your day to take your shoes off, loosen your belt, and just be you. Every time you get sucked into a roundabout of doing and doing, you will inevitably end up in doo-doo! I'm here to remind you to STOP. Take a BE Break. Even if you are crazy-busy, your pee break can include a BE Break.

The "Do-Be-Do-Be-Do-Be" difference empowers you. By managing the level of stress in your body throughout your day, you can avoid the pitfalls and health problems caused by toxic levels of stress hormones.

A good intention for any self-care practice, when not acted upon, can add to your stress levels. Thoughts that start with "I should … take care of my stress" or "I should … eat better" (or anything else that you *should* yourself with) linger in the back of your mind and activate feelings of defeat, guilt, and shame. These feelings can turn you into a bully filled with negative self-talk. "Why can't I just do this? I'm such a loser." Or one I used to use, "It sucks to be me right now." What may seem like harmless comments (like calling yourself "stupid") fuel your motives with disempowering, stress-producing mental programs that run constantly in the back of your mind. "I should do this, I should do that…." They're a lot like open apps running in the background on your cell phone. They drain your battery without you being aware of it. Practice remembering: "I have a choice about how I meet what shows up in my life today. I can *choose* to take a BE Break now to help myself through this rough patch."

There is a deep yearning within each of us to feel good about ourselves, to feel loved. When we feel "less than," or unsure of someone's love, it activates a survival mechanism. "If he needs me, he will love me." It feeds that craving to be needed, to feel indispensable. Unhealthy boundaries or the addiction to saying "yes" to everything and everyone is a lot like eating sugar ... you get a great burst of energy, you may feel needed and loved in that moment ... but then you crash and still feel empty (or worse, resentful) for doing or giving too much.

Wishing for things to be different and feeling like there is nothing you can do about it leaves you feeling powerless, stuck, and exhausted. Do you ever find yourself feeling like there isn't enough time in your day? Or wishing you had more energy? Do you catch yourself dragging your feet in the afternoon, wishing for the day to end? ... And, of course, we all wish for world peace, right?

An occasional yoga student of mine, Betty, came into the studio to say hi. "I'm sorry I haven't had time to come to class," she said. "I'm just so upset about what is happening in this country...." On and on she went, getting all revved up about something she had just heard on the news. "I wish we lived in a world where we could have peace."

"No one seems to be able to invest ten minutes a day for peace in their own body," I said. "If I want world peace, I need to start with myself. Can you find the time to do that for yourself?"

Betty looked at me like I was asking for the moon. Before she started with her grocery list of why it's so hard for her to do that, I looked at her with compassion and said, "Imagine a world where everyone did that." I started singing John Lennon's song, "Imagine."

Betty smiled.

I said something funny to make her laugh.

In that moment, Betty stopped the internal war and the fire of the drama was put out. "I hadn't thought about it that way," she said. "I'll see you in class tomorrow."

Doing something good for yourself or your body can feel hard because there's resistance. The pain of failing at yet another extreme diet or exercise program or another attempt to improve yourself or your life can feed your resistance to making supportive choices. The fear of failure or the bully within you can deflate your confidence to achieve your wellness goals. Let's face it, when the choice comes to being or doing, *doing* wins every time. The Do-Be-Do-Be-Do-Be rhythm gives you another choice. It offers you a way to support your busy lifestyle, to take care of what needs to get done *and* tend to your body's needs throughout your busy day. It gives you a way to turn off the negative self-talk and the self-care "should." It empowers you to take actions that support the whole of you.

When you find yourself losing patience and you feel like you're on an endless uphill stretch with no energy, it's time to stop, pull over, and take a self-care break. When you're feeling stuck or uninspired, you can choose to stay in the struggle—or you can stop and take a moment to recharge your battery and refresh your mind. It's easier to turn the lamp on when it's plugged in. By taking a moment to reconnect to your life force, it's a lot like putting the plug back in the socket. It then becomes easier to turn on your inner Light and get back on track.

It's easier to turn the lamp on when it's plugged in.

Accepting My Gift ~ Embracing My Purpose

Magic happens when we awaken to our purpose. With my propensity toward the spiritual, I knew I was here to serve Spirit in my life. As I shared with you earlier, even as child I felt my life's work was to help others find their inner Light. My thirst for knowledge was (and continues to be) led by my yearning to deepen my own relationship with the Divine or Father~Mother~God of my understanding. I'm not one to accept concepts without questioning. I'm by nature curious and inquisitive. I wonder, "Why? How?" I want to make sense of my mystical experiences. From an early age, I dove deeply into everything that would feed my spiritual growth and help me understand my path to inner peace. Even in grade school, I would walk to school early so I could go to 7:00 a.m. mass at the church conveniently located next door to my school. I loved being in a spiritual place. I felt a peace and a sense of ease there. I couldn't explain it and I never talked about it with the other kids. I was already weird enough with my crazy, curly red hair and overly-freckled face. The kids already had plenty to tease me about. I would walk around the block so nobody would know I was coming to school from church. I often daydreamed about entering a spiritual community (like my aunt Denise, a Franciscan missionary nun, who inspired me so much). The convent seemed like a safe place to live with other spiritually-minded people. When I visited my other retired aunt, Sister Rose, I loved visiting the other sisters at the convent. But soon I became inspired by career goals and distracted by crushes—and somehow becoming a nun never came up as an option in high school. But my quest for learning continues to inspire my ongoing self-healing journey, and it continues to fuel my current work.

After college, in my early twenties, I started my acting career. I secretly thought that perhaps becoming a famous actress would open up my path to helping a lot more people. I thought that by achieving a certain level of success, I'd have the money and influence to make a difference in people's lives in a "Big Way." Fame seemed like a good platform. Oprah was an inspiration. I wanted to share what I was discovering and show others how to tap into their super-powers. I knew we could make the world a better place. But that would have been too easy ... I've always had a knack for finding the path with the most obstacles. I've had a lot practice creating balance the hard way. Partly because I carried the story of the wounded healer. I know now that it's all about healing and releasing my attachments to struggle in this life. The more I maintain my balance, the easier it is to find an effortless path. It starts with a BE Break. Then, I can more easily accept and bless what is showing up and choose the most supportive next step for me in that moment.

My conditioning for survival was particularly strong throughout my twenties and choosing an acting career naturally put me in a game of survival. I was excellent at assessing people's needs in every situation, and this skill helped me get acting work. I was also good at earning people's love and approval by making myself indispensable. Certainly, auditioning required me to be focused on the external, so at times I would focus on keeping up with looking good more than with feeling good. But still, my deep call to the spiritual pulled me out of the physical and nurtured my inner peace. Whenever I got swept up in the drama of a romance or work, I would turn to my deep spiritual connection as a healing balm to heal the wounds of judgment, fear, low self-worth, and other emotional challenges as they came up.

I was booking a lot of commercials, training films, voice-overs, and print jobs, all of which have a lot of on-set waiting time. I would always take a spiritual and inspirational book or two onto the set. Actors deal with rejection daily. The dream of the big break can easily turn into an obsession. It can be easy to lose sight of what is truly important. So, of course, on every set I worked on, there was always an actor or two in need of inspiration and somehow, I always had the perfect book for them with me. My favorite book to pass on was *Illusions: The Adventures of a Reluctant Messiah* by Richard Bach. At that time, in addition to being someone who attracted troubled souls like bees to bee balm, I was just becoming aware of my psychic gift. I would say things that would astound people, about their life, their past, and people in their life that I had no way of knowing.

Word got around and people would come to me with questions about relationships or career: "Can you tell me if I'm going to book the gum commercial?" "Should I look for another agent?" Or, the worst one: "Can you tell me if my boyfriend is cheating on me?" I wasn't yet sure what to do with this clairvoyant gift, but I was clear that I didn't want to use it for fortune-telling. Mostly I was interested in inspiring people to align with their soul's purpose and helping them find their way back to their inner Light. Besides, I didn't really trust my gift to be accurate. I decided to keep my intuitive gift under wraps. At first I thought I could choose to ignore it, but that didn't work. It was like chasing my shadow. I had to accept that it was part of me. So, I made an agreement with Spirit that I would let my intuitive voice speak whenever there was a genuine need.

It took some practice to not let my head get in the way of my intuition. At times I would say things that didn't make any sense to me. I practiced not evaluating any information or trying to make sense of the information that came up. I received a lot of guidance and confirmation that over time made it easier for me to trust that I was being guided to be of service, as a vehicle to inspire and encourage those who were in a dark place in their lives. My intuitive gift really felt like a gift, not a curse. I finally embraced my gift enough to start using the messages I received as part of my healing-and-helping toolkit.

I noticed over time that in the self-help books I was reading, all the words of wisdom about life and death, forgiveness and love were all deeply healing, but it was all inspirational, not actionable. I wanted *more*. For example, on the set of a dental product commercial, my co-actor, Dan, had just received the news that he was in the early stages of lung cancer. He was angry, scared, and overwhelmed with emotions. We were given an hour set change break so we had time alone in the green room. (In show business, the actors' waiting room is called "the green room." If you're curious, the room is almost never green). As I was listening and talking to him in a supportive way, I could feel and even see some of the energy in his body ease a bit. I gave him a few cues that made him start to feel better. It is hard to explain what I was "seeing" because it wasn't in a typical visual way. It was a combination of feeling and seeing where the energy was blocked in his body. As I worked with him, I could "see" his energy begin to flow in a supportive way. He commented that he felt a weight being removed; he could breathe more easily. After he left, I felt like it wasn't enough to be able to make him feel better in the moment. I wanted to know *how I could help him in a more tangible, day-to-day way. I wanted to find a way to help people integrate their harsh physical reality with the sweetness of the spiritual wisdom within the human body.* So many spiritual teachings are about transcending the physical. It's easier when you live away from real-world stress and distraction. But we can't always drop all our obligations, retreat into nature, or go into a retreat center or a spa resort for an extended period of time. Sooner or later, most of us need to return to living and participating in "real life."

I felt that even for me the spiritual was often an escape from the physical. I wanted to find a way to integrate the two and began my quest to discover the physiology of my spirituality. I didn't see Dan for about a year. I was happy to see him turn up at a commercial audition for a foot odor product. He told me that they caught the cancer early and that the surgery was successful. I could tell by his smile that he was feeling better. He shared that after we had talked, his anger had started to subside. He thanked me for the suggestion that he start a gratitude journal; it really worked for him. (And I still recommend it for all my clients)!

Gratitude is one of the most powerful self-healing tools. Dan shared that for him, it was hardest to feel at peace when his body was in physical pain and his mind was overtaken by fear. "I kept reminding myself what you said about this being an opportunity to meet myself with compassion," he said. "I'm still working on that."

Gratitude and compassion are key tools for all of us to keep in our self-healing toolbox. I was thrilled that I had helped Dan in some way. I wanted to understand *how* to support the mind, the intellect, and the entire body to shift out of distress, to make it possible for a human being to be healthy *and* happy. So, I learned everything I could about nutrition. I studied Ayurveda, hypnotherapy, and herbalism while diving deep into the *A Course in Miracles* books, *The Urantia Book*, and many other metaphysical texts. I trained in many self-healing therapies, including color and magnet therapy, meditation, Chi Gong, yoga, and Reiki, to name a few. As I shared earlier, remarkable teachers and masters kept showing up in my life. Being an actor, I was naturally driven to study psychology as well. Happily, the success and flexible schedule of my acting career permitted me to take every opportunity to study self-help psychology and all the holistic self-healing modalities I could find. I studied metaphysics and researched and documented the science behind metaphysical teachings, which later led me to study the Universal Kabbalah, theology, and astrology.

Over time, I became acutely skilled at overcoming the momentary destructive impact of stress on my physical body. I was discovering information about my own food allergies and experiencing the undeniable impact of food on my overall well-being. What a game-changer for me. Beyond just sharing inspirational books and my intuitive insights, I was now able to offer more people more tools to help them. But still, at this stage of my life, my focus on career success was a strong pull. This kept pushing me in and out of periods of drama. It was a bit of a seesaw for me; I was either all about the physical reality and survival or all about the spiritual. The spiritual still felt more like a sweet escape from the physical. I felt divided and was searching for a way to integrate the physical with the spiritual. I wanted to stop the tug-of-war. I was striving for peace, inside and out.

My New York Life ~ The Best and the Worst of Everything

Although by now I was making a good living as an actor, I wasn't breaking into anything big and meaningful. I decided to take a break. I was in between apartments so it was the perfect time to go spend time in New York City, another high-rent city. I felt that there, I could reconnect with why I became an actor. My passion for the craft of acting led me to apply to the Lee Strasberg Institute—and I was accepted into their three-month acting program for film and stage. My 'short New York sabbatical' turned into a thirteen-year adventure during which I had many humbling opportunities to meet stress at a whole other level. I had some of the best and worst experiences—that only New York City (with its population of over seven million people) can foster. I remember when I first arrived. I was standing in the middle of Times Square and I wasn't feeling excited anymore. I was freaking out. The energy, the smells, and the noise were overwhelming. I had to get out of there. Luckily, in New York you can always find a little patch of green in a little park. So, New York was the perfect playground for me to hone my training as a spiritual teacher and stress management coach and now (more specifically), a Do-Do rescue coach. You teach what you need the most. I learned that my inner calling couldn't be about helping others until I had mastered healing myself. It's so much easier to fix others than it is to fix yourself. But just like the in-flight attendants say in the airplane safety speech, you've got to put on your own oxygen mask before you can help others. My New York showbiz life provided a perfect set of circumstances to learn that; it allowed me to live what I now teach.

The thing I remember most is that in the challenging times, I felt like I had no choice. As I explained earlier, that is a symptom of overwhelm ... but I was so deep in my survival story that I didn't even know I was in overwhelm. I was also holding the belief I'd embraced as a little girl that I needed to earn the love of others and prove my self-worth by what I did. I'd never learned how to ask for help, partly because I'd been so disappointed by people in the past. By the age of seventeen I was living on my own and had developed my fiercely independent nature. My motto was always, "The one person I can count on is myself and I can count on the power of God." I didn't know about mantras, but my mother had passed down to me a prayer from my grandmother that worked just like a mantra. I would say it over and over to overcome moments of fear and anxiety. "Mon Jesus, j'vous aime." It means, "My Jesus, I love you," and in French it has a cadence that sounds like a mantra with an "Ommm" in it. It was an effective way for me to feel calm in a storm of fear and anxiety. It worked *every time*. (By this time, I had learned other mantras that helped—and I will share these with you in a moment—but this childhood mantra still comes up from time to time).

> "Some people stand and move
> as if they have no right to the space they occupy.
> They wonder why others often fail to treat them
> with respect— not realizing that they have
> signaled others that it is not necessary to treat
> them with respect."
> ~ **Nathaniel Branden,** *The Six Pillars of Self-Esteem*

I have observed that most stressed-out people are so disconnected from their feelings that they don't even know they are stressed. They feel numb, disconnected from their passion and completely focused on *doing* to avoid *being*. *Overdoing can give you a false sense of empowerment that is rooted in the fear of not being enough.* For me, it was about helping people. I liked helping people; it was a quick and easy way for me to feel better about myself. But the fear of "being" and the stress of constant "doing" can create a subtle poison in your body that can only be ignored until a life and/or health crisis shows up that stops you in your tracks. That became true for me during my time living in New York City.

An expert survivor, I had always found a way to push through life's demands. I never thought of myself as an overdoer or as a stressed-out person. After all, I was a deeply spiritual person who practiced meditation. I had self-care routines like yoga and Chi Gong organically integrated into my life. As noted, I was (and still am) a holistic health coach and yoga teacher, and at one time, I was an aerobics instructor. I was disciplined and I knew a lot about being fit and maintaining a healthy lifestyle. I was also the classic "Miss Independent" ... just like in Kelly Clarkson's song.

When I left Toronto I had ended a long relationship with a man (John) who was a soul mate. We had a strong, loving spiritual connection. John asked me to marry him. I said yes! We decided to live together. I was in no rush to get married so we waited to set a wedding date. After years of living together, although it felt safe and easier to stay with John, I knew that he wasn't the man I was to marry in this life. We both had other things to learn, things that I couldn't learn with him or he with me. It became clear that I had to go away so we could fulfill our souls' journeys in this life. As long as we lived close to each other, the pull back to each other would get in the way. The Universe orchestrated the circumstances—I just needed to listen to my inner guidance and follow my spirit through the struggle of our hearts breaking.

John was my first experience of true unconditional love. It was a challenge to match that kind of love in my other relationships. After every other breakup, I often feared that being with John had been my one shot at true unconditional love—and I'd blown it. I'm grateful to say it wasn't—but that's a story for another book. When you surrender to your Higher good and the Higher good of others, the Universe can play its part to create the circumstances. For me, it was an opportunity to go to New York City. It felt exciting, the call was magnetic, and I was able to resolve all the obstacles that stood in my way of making it happen. John even insisted on driving me to New York from Toronto via Montreal so I could say "au revoir" to my family. He knew I was following my soul path even though he didn't completely understand it. That's what unconditional love does. What a gift he has been in my life!

When I got to New York, a relationship was the last thing I was interested in. Of course, that is always when the opportunities show up, right? When I first got there, I was living in a dorm room at the Vanderbilt Y. I had never really dated more than one person at a time, but since I was set on not getting into a relationship, I took some opportunities to date a few interesting New Yorkers that eager matchmaker friends introduced me to. One date picked me up in a chauffeur-driven car. Another date drove a little Mercedes, and another took me on a subway ride—each of them came to pick me up at the Y. It felt like I was in a sitcom TV show; I was having fun. I was set on not getting involved, so nothing came of any of these dates.

Living in my tiny room at the Y became unbearable. This was before cellphones so the lineup to make phone calls was endless. Messages were sometime slipped under the door, sometimes not. It was very hard to keep in touch with the outside world. I was also aware that my money was dwindling. I was sharing my concern with one of my classmates, Suzy, as we were walking out of scene class. She invited me to have a drink with her at the bar of a nice Italian restaurant around the corner from the school. Suzy was gorgeous and was attracting a lot of attention. The manager brought us drinks from a customer. Suzy was used to this. I was a bit shy and uncomfortable but this was her plan of "taking me" for a drink. I noticed the manager's accent and started to speak French with him. Out of the blue, he asked me if by any chance I needed a job. They were looking for a part-time hostess. I thought it was a joke. But we set up an interview for the next afternoon. And I had a part-time job!

A few weeks later, the same manager, André, again out of the blue asked, "Do you know anyone who is looking for an apartment? My neighbor down the hall just told me she is looking for a new roommate."

"Wow," I thought," This is too good to be true." I called and met with her. She was great; we hit it off *and* the apartment and the price were perfect for me. She offered me a cute loft bed "room" in the living room with a big closet underneath, and the building had a doorman. What more does a girl need? It cost just about the same as my room at the Y and it was walking distance to school and work. Things were manifesting for me to have a full experience of living in the Big Apple.

I liked working at the restaurant. Part of my compensation was an early dinner that I could order off their lunch menu before my 5:00 p.m. shift. I was meeting interesting people. The customer base was mostly successful New Yorkers, including celebrities. Every Friday they had live music. One particular night, they had a trio: singer, piano, and bass. That's when it happened—I fell in love again. This time the connection was not spiritual, but Ed was a very talented musician and it was a creative and electric attraction. After three months of dating, it started to turn into a serious relationship that motivated me to stay in New York after my acting program ended. I had a good living situation and work, so it was easy. The relationship grew over several months until we decided we were ready to live together.

By this time I was working as a holistic practitioner teaching Reiki classes all over New York, New Jersey, and Pennsylvania, while still pursuing work as an actor. To support my decision to stay in New York, I got a regular job with a software company as a sales and customer support rep. I was not sure where my life was going, juggling the job with my acting and spiritual work. Before long, my spiritual work became my main work, and the lack of spiritual connection in my relationship became more of an issue. I began to feel like I couldn't really be myself. I started to feel like I couldn't breathe.

Ed and I lived in a small ... I mean *tiny* ... apartment on the fifth floor of a walkup building in a busy neighborhood called Hell's Kitchen. I was walking up and down those stairs with my massage table to go teach workshops or to work on clients, and fighting my way down the busy avenue. There were so many wonderful things about this area that I loved, but I was feeling lost. Day by day, the spiritual disconnect between Ed and me became more and more of a dividing factor. It became clear that it was time once again to surrender to my soul's calling—it was time for the relationship to end.

I moved in with a wonderful roommate, Wanda, who had a huge rent-controlled apartment on the Upper West Side. It took me five cab rides to get all my stuff moved in. I loved the Upper West Side. I was enjoying living in New York in a whole new way. I felt broken and was now in a wonderful place to mend the pieces of my heart. I was now passionate about NOT looking for a relationship.

Then I met Jake.

THE FABLE OF MISS INDEPENDENT

One of my clients shared with me that she was amazed at how much her healing sessions with me, along with a 12-Step program, had helped her with her recovery from alcoholism. I knew very little about recovery, but I had heard great things about 12-Step programs. She suggested that I go to an open meeting, which non-members could attend, and see for myself what it was all about.

I was curious, so I went to an open meeting. The room was packed, full of chatter. A welcoming greeter directed me to where the coffee was. The room went impressively silent as soon as it started. After the meeting, someone came up to me and asked me if this was my Day One. "What?" I hadn't thought about myself as having a drinking problem, but the stories I heard that day struck a chord. The speaker at the meeting also talked about denial. If I say "no" to counting days, am I in denial? I went home and felt the depth of the emotional pain I was in. I needed to do something and recovery felt like a possible answer. I started going to meetings in my new neighborhood for people in recovery. I started counting days. As a healer, I wanted to understand more about the power of 12-Step programs and as an actress, I was eager to jump into the experience and learn more about the psychology of recovery. The stories shared and the characters in them fascinated me. The meetings felt at times like what I imagined group therapy to be ... and at other times, it was a place to bring emotional support and spiritual inspiration to others. Not drinking wasn't that hard for me (I did have one good drinking story from high school to share), but it felt like a big deal because I was going through an unhappy time. I could relate to the experience of emotional struggle that permeated everyone's stories.

As long as I was willing to label myself as "in recovery," the group welcomed me as one of them. I was completely focused on healing my heart and all the pieces of my broken-self. Not drinking felt like a supportive choice and the meetings gave me a reason to get dressed and get out of my apartment. New York is a city that can make you feel like a drop of water stuck in a jar floating in an ocean. It's a weird kind of lonely. I felt accepted and happy to be part of this courageous group of people and I enjoyed sharing and making new friends. As far as alcoholism went, I used the fact that I liked having a glass of wine with dinner and I missed it especially during this period of heartache. It felt like a good, healthy challenge not to drink at this time.

Looking back, what I was struggling with wasn't so much the glass of wine, but finding my way back to myself. Not drinking removed any masking of my feelings. I was "all in," which led me to explore several other 12-Step programs. I learned a lot about addiction and co-dependent relationships. I'm grateful for all I learned about the human condition and addiction. We all have some level of addiction to something: Facebook, a game, work, shopping ... potato chips ... something we use to numb or distract ourselves from uncomfortable feelings and challenges. The surprising one for me (that I discovered later in my life) was my addiction to struggle. It was so familiar to me, it put me in my comfort zone.

There was a lot of wisdom in those rooms and I loved the spiritual part of the 12-Step programs. I was in a sagacious period of self-discovery and self-healing. Breakups have always been rich healing opportunities for me, a way to get to know myself at a deeper level. Being in the group, I was learning about being vulnerable and open about my challenging feelings. I was experiencing receiving unconditional support, something I was skilled at giving but not so good at receiving. I didn't know many people in New York and at the meetings I found other people who were interested in spirituality (not everyone was) and who were committed to improving their lives. I noticed that those who resisted the spiritual part had a more difficult time staying sober and remained at war with their addiction. The people in the support group welcomed me and my words of inspiration. I wasn't into going to bars and drinking and I enjoyed hanging out with sober people. I also felt needed and appreciated. It may sound strange but it was a lot like going to church for me. Showing up held an emotional reward for making the effort and I loved reciting the "Serenity Prayer" with the group.

After several months of going to regular neighborhood meetings, my friend group continued to expand. I was constantly meeting new, interesting people who, like me, were not into drinking, one day at a time. As we were leaving a birthday party gathering, a man named Jake asked me to go out for coffee. I turned him down. I wasn't interested in dating and didn't want to encourage the possibility. He was charming and handsome, in a Marlborough Man sort of way. We stood outside for a while and talked. It turned out that we lived in the same neighborhood and we had a lot in common. I enjoyed talking with him and we ended up going for coffee. He was a working actor who had turned his life around in a positive way. He was full of interesting stories. Neighborhoods in New York are small and we kept running into each other. He would suggest meeting at various neighborhood restaurants for dinner and before long, we were dating.

The relationship escalated quickly. There was a strong attraction, but looking back, I realize now that it was my "Miss Independent" persona that attracted him. We started spending weekends together at his country place. Jake had just renovated it and I jumped in to help him with decorating and setting things up to make it homey. He was older than anyone I had ever dated (there was a twenty-year age difference). But he was more energetic and fun than some of the younger guys I had dated in the past.

Being together was easy. Jake shared with me that he had a dream of becoming a father and just like many of our daydreams, we talked about it ... for the future. Then unexpectedly, the dream became a reality. I was shocked because I was very careful and responsible about this kind of stuff. Of course, the relationship had become serious but it was still a shock. Be careful what you wish for.

In a meditation, I had a revelation that this little soul was a miracle, destined to be here. I felt such love and purpose in my heart and soul. I knew beyond a doubt that I was destined to be his mother.

This was not a planned pregnancy, so there were a lot of emotional adjustments all around. Jake was consumed with fear and doubt. This didn't change my assured feeling. I felt the support of my friends; especially my roommate, Wanda, who had become a soul sister. And, my mother was there for me. I was so grateful because I was experiencing an unfamiliar feeling—I had *never* felt so vulnerable in my life.

Once Jake decided to be part of this journey with me, he was extremely supportive. As we were settling into the pregnancy, I gave myself permission to indulge in self-care in a way I had never done before. It felt necessary for my baby's sake. I made a greater effort to eat the best food, when I could eat. I felt nauseous and tired all the time. I was uncontrollably emotional ... and did I mention *vulnerable*? Wow, that was not a comfortable feeling for me. And with the struggle to keep going as "Do-Do" girl, I couldn't keep up. For the first time in my adult life, I took naps. I also made more time for meditation and, of course, I went to pre-natal exercise classes. The recovery meetings were becoming less and less a part of my life. My focus was my pregnancy and I surrounded myself with loving, supportive, close friends and other pregnant women ... especially Alyia, whom I had met in a hospital pre-natal class. She was a few months ahead of me in her pregnancy. She was here from Australia because her husband was on assignment and she, like me, didn't have family in New York. Our favorite thing to do was to go to this amazing olive bar in her neighborhood on the Upper East Side. The best olives! Our favorites were green and the size of a plum. We loved meeting for lunch and sharing about our pregnancies.

After my first trimester, I was feeling better, so I became more focused on getting things ready for the baby. Frankly, once I'd stopped throwing up and I'd passed my first trimester, I felt like I could keep doing what I had always done. I also tried to keep up doing what Jake loved to do—fishing. There I was, helping to lift the canoe up onto the car. I was "doing it all" until the end of my fourth month, when I felt more lower pressure in my belly.

When I saw the doctor, he informed me that the pressure I was feeling was premature labor symptoms. I was put on moderate bed rest. I couldn't believe it. I was terrified about the consequences this would have on my relationship. I had just moved in with Jake. The independent, self-sufficient person that Jake had pursued was gone. But, he surprised me with a lot of support ... and a marriage proposal.

Not being able to do is not easy. I managed to rest as much as I could because I was scared for our baby's safety. It was hard, but being pregnant gave me the strength and purpose to get through it.

After our son, Derick, was born six weeks prematurely, there was nothing left of my "Miss Independent" persona. I experienced a whole other level of vulnerability and low self-confidence. I was totally focused on Derick, my marriage to Jake, my social obligations, and trying to meet the needs of my new family. Jake still had his dream house in the country and a contract in a TV show. His schedule was random, he worked any given two to four days in a week, depending on the storyline of his character. I spent my time packing and unpacking to go up to the country based on his schedule.

It was hard to both schedule activities for Derick *and* do anything for myself. I gave up trying to go back to work and was grateful to be a stay-at-home-mom. I was driven by my need to meet the expectations of being the perfect mother and the perfect wife. Jake was mostly a supportive husband, a great provider, and there was baby-magic in those early months of being new parents. Everything else seemed unimportant.

I had spent the first two weeks after giving birth going across town to the hospital to be with Derick, holding and rocking him. But they would not let me breastfeed, so I pumped every three hours or more. When I got home, I pumped to express breast milk every four hours to keep up my supply! I even set an alarm to wake up in the night to pump when Derick was still in the hospital. Nursing a preemie was challenging and painful, but I was determined and I stuck to it. It was amazing to me that something that is supposed to be so natural could be so hard. It's common for hospitals to encourage moms with preemie babies to bottle-feed them at birth, thus, often preemies don't learn to latch on to the breast properly. With preemie babies, it seems to be all about the baby's weight gain. At this point, breastfeeding alone was a full-time job ... but totally worth it for baby and me. Derick's immune system was strong and I was back in my skinny jeans in no time.

But I had totally lost sight of my inner balance. I was all in with the doing and doing, yet somehow always feeling that I wasn't doing enough. I was focused on keeping things happy and harmonious for my family. I loved preparing delicious meals. For me it was a great way to nurture my family. I had access to the best fresh ingredients at my local markets, and we visited our favorite local restaurants, all within a few blocks of our co-op apartment ... one of the things I loved about living in New York City. When we were in the country, I made fresh breads, pies, and heart-warming, home-cooked meals. My husband was into it. I had always been pretty fearless at trying things, but I found myself second-guessing myself at everything. Jake happens to be great at everything he does, and he was kind enough to point out all the things I needed to improve ... like the way I was tying my shoelaces was all wrong until he showed me the way! He taught me so many things ... I always felt a certain pressure to meet his expectations. But the one thing I could not be made wrong about was being my son's mother. Especially as his red hair started to grow in!

As time went on, my baby's needs continued to increase and though I often had the thought that I "should" meditate, I rarely had the time. I would intend to do a bit of yoga stretching while playing with Derick on the floor, but the focus was always on his needs and—as all mothers know—babies are a full-time job. I often prayed myself to sleep, and in those moments I felt my connection to divine peace. During my times of struggle with breastfeeding, I would call on the grace of God to give me the strength to be the best mother for Derick. It gave me the strength to keep going.

My first "date" with Jake after giving birth, without our now-four-month-old baby, was to the Emmy awards. Jake was a nominee! I had no family in New York and none of my friends had babies. The thought of getting a babysitter was overwhelming. We were so grateful when my mom came all the way from Montreal to babysit for us.

I looked great in my size two gown with the deep-cut, sequined top that revealed the best cleavage of my life (especially by the end of Emmy night, thanks to my baby-food boobs). The limo let us off at the wrong entrance, so we had to run down one block to catch another limo to make the red-carpet entrance. I was grateful that my choice of shoes was not three-inch stilettos. We made a great red carpet entrance, albeit a little out of breath. As we were mingling in the theatre before the show, I noticed I was having trouble taking a breath in without coughing. There I was, in a room with some of the industry's top people, and I couldn't say a single word without coughing. I was a few feet away from Oprah and as I was about to meet her, I had to move away abruptly because I started coughing. We got the cue that the show was about to start and we had to go to our assigned seats, near the front with the other nominees. I was trying not to cough as the camera focused on the nominees to catch reaction shots. Thankfully, I managed not to cough long enough for Jake's camera moment. I really thought he deserved to win, but he didn't. It was a fun night for the most part, but my ribs were hurting from coughing. I was anxious to get home. I was on the verge of overflowing; I needed to nurse my baby.

Over the next few weeks, that involuntary, nonproductive dry cough kept coming back and then wouldn't go away. It got so I couldn't take a deep breath or even speak without a little involuntary cough that sounded like a fake cough. I was shocked to hear, at the age of thirty, my doctor's diagnosis of asthma. I didn't know you could develop asthma. My school friend Lucie had almost died from it. The doctor mentioned that my asthma was stress-induced, but I didn't think I was that stressed; I was just getting used to being a mom. He said that not getting enough rest combined with seasonal allergies could exacerbate the problem but that I would feel better by using inhalers as needed. So, I carried on with what I thought was a busy but healthy lifestyle ... I kept going with my busy New York life.

One day, I was in the kitchen in our country house, alone with baby Derick, making dinner. The unproductive cough had started up in the previous few days. It was just annoying and not severe ... or so I thought. In this moment, I kept doing what I was doing, intending to look for my inhaler as soon as I was done with cooking. We had company coming for dinner and I wanted to get the pie in the oven so it would be ready on time. But the cough escalated into wheezing, and turned into a coughing attack. Over my kitchen sink, I braced myself, panicked, helpless, unable to take a breath. I flashed back to my childhood experience when I'd stopped breathing. I was scared, but as I braced myself I felt light around me and the warmth of a hand between my shoulder blades. I heard a voice in my head say, "Louise, stay calm." I reached for a glass of water. I was gasping loudly for air. Then, as I relaxed, I was able to start taking gentle breaths again.

Not being able to breathe definitely got my attention. I realized that I was navigating my life in the dark. It felt like I was coming out of a long power failure and the lights had just come back on. I realized I had lost my way to my Light switch. I was seeing my life and myself with a whole new awareness and for the first time in a long time, I let go. I cried. Like a wild summer rain, crying seemed to cleanse my spirit.

At that moment, I stopped trying to keep it all together and I let myself feel how disconnected I was from my deep soul-self. After a deep puff of my inhaler, I took Derick in my arms and sat in the rocking chair, grateful to be breathing again. Looking into his deep blue eyes, I felt an overwhelming mama-love for this tiny being. I needed to take care of myself so I could be here for him. For the first time since my NDE (the Near-Death Experience I shared with you earlier), I really wanted to be here. I was determined to create more balance in my day; I would take time for myself during his baby naps.

Every "good" thing I was doing for my health and well-being was about changing myself, instead of healing myself.

As Derick turned into an energetic toddler, the naps got shorter. We spent more time at the park and out in nature. That was so nurturing for both of us. I got more sleep through the night and felt like I was getting myself back. But I was still carrying the burden of trying to be the perfect wife, and frankly, I didn't even know what that looked like. My self-worth was tied to what I did or didn't get done. Thinking back, because perfection is not possible, I was feeling bad about myself most of the time. Every "good" thing I was doing for my health and well-being was about changing myself instead of healing myself. The only thing I felt good about was being Derick's mom. I felt I was failing at my marriage—and that terrified me. I had never been in a relationship where I felt so inadequate all the time. In any other circumstance, I would probably have walked away from this feeling of insecurity. But now I was a mom. I wanted to keep our family together. That was more important to me than feeling better about myself.

When we spent time in the country, I felt isolated. Derick was now too energetic to come along in the backpack child carrier, so most days Jake would go fishing on his own or with other fishing friends, or he was busy doing his own thing. Miss Independent had turned into an old-fashioned housewife, taking care of the house and our toddler, waiting for my husband to come home for dinner. The glue of our relationship and my raison d'être was my beautiful little baby boy. Derick's ongoing growth and milestones were a daily source of delight and laughter that—most days—outshone my sadness.

Baby love is powerful. But it changes as a baby turns into a toddler. While the love between child and parent continued to grow beyond what I could ever have imagined, the baby-glue of our marriage was thinning.

After the birth of a child, a couple enters into a unique love bubble that seems to fade as their baby gets older. That was true for my relationship, which was delicate from the beginning. I remember thinking, "This is a familiar feeling, this feeling of walking on eggshells." I never knew how Jake was going to react in any given moment. It reminded me of how I felt around my father. Jake is a brilliant, gifted man. I had become accustomed to the fact that it was useless to

Do-Do Rescue

argue any point with him for fear of stepping on an emotional land mine. Frankly, I had become doubtful of *all* my abilities. Yet somehow, we had become a loving, beautiful family. In full color, in the magazines, our life in the country looked picture-perfect. People would often complement Jake on his beautiful family. At first it made him smile with pride and joy. But I could see it was no longer a source of joy for him. I didn't know what to do ... or who to be.

My life story was being played into the storyline of Jake's TV character. It was a little surreal—though at first it was fun. When we met, Jake's character had a winter-summer romance budding on the show, much like ours. Then his co-star was pregnant in real life and they wrote her pregnancy into the show. When I got pregnant, I turned to her for advice for an OB-GYN doctor. When I showed up for my first appointment, the receptionist said enthusiastically, "Your husband's girlfriend is having her baby here too!"

"I know," I replied joyfully, "she's the reason I'm here." I walked into the waiting room with everyone looking at me in shock. I just sat down and smiled. Only in New York could that scenario play out!

But now, there was trouble being played out on the TV screen and I was feeling the echo in our lives as well. Most days I woke up with a feeling of dread. I would ease it by breathing and saying a gratitude prayer, and before long I was into the day in full Do-Do mode. Everything seemed okay enough to keep going. My self-care practices were on a long list of "shoulds" that only made me feel bad about myself. But I was too busy trying to keep up to do anything about self-care. I felt like if I stopped, I would drown. I thought I had to keep going, to keep my head above water.

Jake was for the most part a caring husband and loving father. But he was restless. After months of couple's therapy, he announced that he was no longer attracted to me. He wanted a divorce. Ouch! We had decided to sell the city apartment and country house. We had just spent six months renovating our dream house forty miles outside the city. He encouraged me not to move out of the city because it would be so much easier for me to rekindle my acting career if I stayed in New York. I had a close friend who was in the process of subletting her two-bedroom Upper West Side apartment. I called her in the nick of time ... it was still available. With Jake's encouragement, I moved in two weeks later.

I felt like I was at the bottom of a hole that I had dug myself into. I had neglected my relationship with myself by trying to hold on to a relationship with Jake. I realized, "I'm not attracted to me either." When you get lost in Do-Do mode, you stink! I had to surrender. There was nothing I could do to fix this. You can't make someone love you.

The truth was that I wasn't happy being in a relationship in which I felt invisible and devalued. It was time to stop trying not to drown and time to swim to shore. Even though I wanted to hold on to our marriage for my son (and because of the pain of my parent's divorce), I knew I needed to heal myself inside and out. I needed to get my body and my life into balance. I was exhausted from my fruitless efforts to meet Jake's expectations, trying to be perfect from the outside. After we ended our couple's therapy, I continued to see a therapist to get help in reclaiming the broken pieces of myself again. This time, my self-worth was shattered. I was ready to face the connections to my childhood wounds.

The breakup left me feeling like I wasn't good enough. It was humbling. I felt even more insecure about my abilities and physical appearance. With all the demands of running after an active toddler and the stress of the separation, I'd lost so much weight, I was now scary skinny. I also felt like a failure. I realized that what I was most upset about was that I had allowed my inner Light to go out. External demands are the loudest when they define our self-worth. I thought my internal well-being would take care of itself organically, as it had in the past. It clearly needed my attention. It was time to rekindle my relationship with my spirit and my soul-self. Therapy helped me get some much-needed clarity.

When a relationship ends, often there are two different points of view on how and why it didn't work. It can be hurtful and frustrating. The important thing for me wasn't to justify my point of view. I used my therapy sessions to focus on my part in the story and heal what I was willing to accept about myself. I got so much from the work I did over three years, both with our couple's therapist and my personal therapist. They both helped me face some truths about my part in the relationship and about myself—including the fact that I didn't have a problem with alcohol and that I needed to heal the hurt I'd experienced as a child. I was taking responsibility for who I had become. The gifts of taking on a grown-up role at such a young age were all part of my childhood survival story—they had given me a wounded strength. But now, I could reclaim my inner power and become an empowered healer for myself and my life.

My divorce proceedings with Jake echoed my childhood experience of my parents' divorce. But through it all, for me, a peaceful resolution was more important than fighting to be right or for money. When you have children, you can dissolve the marriage but not the partnership of parenting. My main focus was for us to come out of divorce court as good co-parents. It wasn't always easy. My lawyer commented that in all the years he had been a divorce lawyer, he had never met a more reasonable ex-wife. I was clear that I didn't want Derick to experience the anguish I did during my parents' divorce. It was hard enough for him to adjust to the new living arrangement. I fought for Derick to be taken care of, but peace in his little heart was more important to me than being right. I valued Jake as Derick's dad. What was best for Derick was for him to know that he was loved and supported by both his parents. This has paid off for all of us in the long run. Jake's commitment to being a good dad to Derick made it easier for us to make co-parenting possible. I am so grateful to him for that. Managing my stress during that time wasn't always easy for me.

Being aware that Do-Do mode can happen is one thing, but not falling back into it can be challenging. Beyond therapy, what deepened my emotional healing journey was my rekindled commitment to my spiritual practices. If it hadn't been for my yoga, Chi Gong, and meditation practices, I don't think I would have survived the impact on my health from the stress of the divorce. It helped me clear and heal the resentments, the anger, and the calamitous sadness I felt. I was still struggling for balance and I continued to fall in and out of Do-Do mode—but I wasn't stuck in it anymore.

Entering the stressful reality of being a single parent was mind-boggling at times. Just as our divorce became final, I noticed that Derick wasn't talking as much. His pre-school teacher encouraged me to have him tested. He was diagnosed as having Pervasive Development Disorder. *What is that?* I went to Barnes & Noble and looked through books. Finally, I found a definition: *autism*. What? I'd once known of a child with autism who didn't talk at all and banged his head rhythmically against a wall. That was not my Derick. My son had been an early talker, he was full of joy. Then, it just stopped. Was it the divorce? How could this be? Having a child on the autism spectrum took me into a whole new world of parenting. None of the parenting books had prepared me for this. I was grateful that I had tools and self-healing techniques to help me cope.

I embraced Derick's diagnosis. Jake did not ... at first. He thought it was just me stressing Derick out. But, after hearing from professionals, Jake finally got behind me in finding the best support for Derick. Derick had some impressive tantrums, in daunting and impossible settings ... almost always on a busy New York City street. The episode I remember most was on a cold, late afternoon, in rush hour, outside a Fairway food market. Derick threw himself down on the crowded sidewalk. I tried and tried to get him up, but he would not budge. I picked him up off the sidewalk, he was kicking and screaming, "Don't take me away!" I feared that someone would call the police; happily, no one did. But I needed to dig deep, calling on all my stress relief training to access a deep well of patience. Transitions were hard for Derick. Often, when it was time to leave a place like the bookstore or the park, he would scream and refuse to get into the stroller. Sometimes, getting on the bus wasn't happening either. I once carried him, the groceries, and his stroller over ten blocks. I had a lot of opportunities to practice my stress reduction techniques so I could stay calm in the moment. Not easy. And I admit, I did not do this perfectly most of the time.

We took the advice of the neurologist who evaluated Derick and got him into a language intensive school for kids on the spectrum. Getting Derick help at an early age was the best thing we could have done. Derick thrived in his new school. It gave him a supportive approach to learning that tended to his special needs. It offered music therapy and occupational therapy and gave me a great source of support to cope with his needs. The best advice I got in dealing with these difficult situations was: "You do what you need to do to keep your child safe. Forget about what other people say." I was managing, but I still felt like I was juggling most of the time.

As Derick got older, I started to try and restore my acting career. It was a struggle. It's a whole other reality having to show up for auditions to play the TV mom when you're a real mom. Saying lines for a cough syrup commercial, looking like a real-life, sleep-deprived mom with bags under my eyes didn't get me the job. Then, I had to turn down parts that required me to be out of town. Turning down movie parts was hard. I was cast in an off-Broadway showcase production. Keeping up with my son and rehearsal was challenging and yes, stressful. I was having more asthma incidents. It was hard to breathe at times, even with the inhalers. During this particular stress of juggling rehearsal, work, and Derick, I lost my voice. I only had a one-night performance and casting directors were coming. I didn't want to miss the show and let the cast members and my then-agent down. The doctor gave me a cortisone shot and told me that if I didn't stop and rest after the show, I would end up in the hospital. I got through the performance—barely—and I didn't get any calls from casting agents. My work and health were failing. Clearly, I was still struggling with balance in my life. I recommitted again to doing my yoga practice almost daily.

The yoga practice worked at improving my health and opened up opportunities for me! By the time my son was a six-year-old, I had very little need for inhalers. I was also spending more time on my sound meditation practice, to balance the ups and downs of my life. It propelled me to learn more about the ancient practices and the impact of sound on the human body. There was no online yoga at the time. A friend had given me a series of six audio tapes of Kundalini yoga practices with a booklet and I used it every day. I had started to practice Kundalini yoga a long time ago when I was still in Toronto. I loved it. I noticed my breathing was always better after I did a practice and I was able to meet the challenges of my day without losing my sense of humor.

I continued to practice my yoga even when I didn't have time for the full ninety minutes. I broke it down into shorter sections or I would choose a supportive meditation to deal with the stressful situation of the moment.

My New York City life continued to be stressful, but I felt more balanced. Finally, I was living from the inside out. I was still struggling to make time to meditate every morning, but I was committed to my spiritual journey. One day, after a sleepless night with Derick suffering from an ear infection, I called my agent to cancel yet another audition. At that moment, it hit me ... being a working actor didn't fit with the kind of mothering experience I wanted with my son. I began to release this dream that no longer fit in with the quality of life I wanted for us. Letting this dream go was harder than I thought it would be. I released it daily for the first few weeks, letting it go with love and gratitude—and a few tears. Making supportive choices with the intention of creating a peaceful and balanced life for my son and myself was a tremendous navigational compass. I knew I was once again following my inner guidance. I felt at peace and ready to create the next adventure in my life.

This was also a time when I began to ask myself a question that shifted my self-healing practices. As I shared earlier, I realized that *a lot of the inner work I was doing was about trying to change myself instead of healing myself.* I began to practice being in a more compassionate, healing relationship with myself. I asked myself, "Do you want to be perfect or peaceful?" It was clear to me that these two things could not coexist. I realized that I couldn't feel at peace if I was continually judging and "shoulding" myself. I needed to get fear out of the driver's seat of my life at a deeper level.

Looking for work gave me plenty of opportunities to practice self-love in a big way. I was facing all the feelings triggered by fear of the unknown. During my meditations, I was able to feel how powerful that doorway of the unknown can be when fear is not directing the show. But I was still in a tug-of-war between the demands of my busy life, paying the bills, and the sweetness of inner peace. I had to forcefully put fear in the back seat several times a day by breathing and doing short yogic practices to alleviate the stress and clear the anxious feelings moment by moment. Peace doesn't make all your problems magically disappear, but it does create healing space in your body so you can have more clarity to make supportive choices.

The Do-Be-Do-Be-Do-Be Stress Test

After Jake and I had lived forty miles apart for the first two years after our divorce, Jake moved back into the city. Then my sublet came to an end and I needed to find a place to live. I wasn't having any luck renting an apartment I could afford. For each apartment that could work, there were several applicants and being a single mother, I lost out. Jake told me that an apartment was available for purchase in his co-op building. Through a series of miracles, I was able to buy it.

We were happy to be able to work out the best co-parenting solution by living in the same building. Derick knew that his dad was on the fifth floor and his mom on the tenth. We had a few awkward moments but for the most part it was great for Derick. Jake and I were both focused on Derick's well-being and we had a good co-parenting relationship. We attended school events together and occasionally did family outings together. When he was gone for extended periods of time doing an out-of-town show, I would take Derick to see him. As the number of divorced parents at the school increased over the years, people marveled at how harmonious our relationship was.

Two years later, Jake announced that he was moving to another borough and encouraged me to consider moving there too. I had just let go of being an actor. I was thinking about Derick being ready to transition into a regular public school, which would have been challenging in my current neighborhood. I wasn't feeling the need to stay in Manhattan, so I told Jake I was willing to explore the possibilities. I asked a friend to drive up there with me and I was delighted to feel into the possibility of living in a more peaceful environment near a good public school. I was also motivated to continue to make the co-parenting experience easier for our son.

At this time, I was using my meditation practice to activate my inner magnet, to attract what would support Derick's (and my) Higher good. First, I got a new job. I was hired to be national marketing director for a company out of Newport Beach. I could work from home but the job required me to travel two nights a week for some of the time. Derick was spending one or two nights at his dad's every week. Perhaps we could make that work. It was such a perfect job for me, and frankly, it was the only job offer I had that could potentially pay well, with medical *and* dental. I wanted to make it work. I sold my apartment myself in one weekend, with one Sunday *New York Times* ad. I found a great co-op apartment that happened to be just a block away from Jake's new home. The work days I needed Jake to take Derick didn't work for him so I had to hire a full-time childcare person. That was one of the hardest things, but I had a wonderful babysitter who was a mother and a grandmother. She was willing to work overnights. I was manifesting all the pieces at a rapid rate. All of these events: the move, starting a new job, setting up childcare, buying a new apartment (which needed some renovations, of course), buying a car—it all unfolded within a two-month period.

Any one of these things would have been stressful enough, but juggling all of them at the same time was intense. I was also handling the pressures of being a working mom—it was stressful to be away (especially with childcare worries) and to arrange my busy work schedule to be there for Derick and attend all school events! It had become impossible for me to find short or long periods for any kind of practice, but I started to sprinkle some yogic and Chi Gong practices throughout my day. I found that short periods of practicing some of the breathing techniques and modified exercises helped me not only to feel more balanced, but also enabled me to perform better at my job. I had created a way to practice yoga on the go ... whether I was sitting in my car, waiting at the airport, or waiting for a meeting; I could do yoga and no one around me knew what I was doing. I managed my stress levels within the reality and the demands of any given moment. I was able to manage my obligations, be devoted to my son, and I was enjoying my life and being me. I was feeling the power of being in the driver's seat of my life.

CHAPTER 3
DO-DO RESCUE: THE DO-BE-DO-BE-DO-BE SOLUTION

It's easy to blame external circumstances for your stress and upset. It's true that you may not always be able to control what other people do that affects you. But you always have a choice about how you react and meet these situations. Taking supportive action in the moment will empower you not to fall into victim mode. When you take a BE Break, you are in the driver's seat of that moment. It's like defensive driving—you can make choices that will get you out of harm's way. You will feel grounded and calm so you can take control of your life experience.

When your day and your life become only about trying to keep up with external demands, when you are always "shoulding" on yourself—saying "I should do this" or "I should do that," it's a clue that you are walking into Do-Do. As I said earlier, where there's a "should," there's a shame story, or a fear-based motive that doesn't serve you. Start by giving yourself permission, right now, to let that go. Reframe every "should" with a choice: "I choose to take a moment to breathe." Let go of perfection and make space in your day to enjoy just being you.

Every time you get sucked onto the hamster wheel of doing and doing, you will inevitably end up in Do-Do. I'm here to remind you: STOP—get off. Take a BE Break. The solution to avoiding overwhelm is to manage your stress levels throughout your day. Consult this book whenever you need to, and rely on its techniques and strategies ... not only to help you lower your stress levels, but also to help you align with choices that support you and your highest good. By taking strategic BE Breaks, you can enjoy more energy, less pain, and less fatigue in your body, mind, and spirit.

In this section, we'll address taking care of *All of You* ... by guiding you into connecting with your whole being ... from your belly to your Mind to your Heart.

SIDE EFFECTS

With the Do-Be-Do-Be-Do-Be lifestyle, you will feel less stress and have more energy to get things done. One of the side effects I have discovered is that my clients often get the irresistible urge to smile—they feel happy for no reason. For example, one day I got a call from one of my New York clients. She was in a panic.

"I was getting ready to go to work today," she said. "I noticed that I was smiling. I couldn't help it."

"That's great," I said.

"No, you don't understand," she said, agitated. "I had no reason to smile. What's wrong with me?"

I reassured her. "You are experiencing a side effect of inner peace. When you are used to feeling stressed out all the time, at first it can feel a little disconcerting to feel good. Don't skip your BE Breaks. That's an old habit that keeps you stuck. It will get easier with time, so give yourself a chance, and stick to it. You will see that not only your body, but your life starts to feel more joyful."

If you can't wait for this to be you—the authentic, empowered you, who feels happy for no reason and smiles "just because"—read on!

Your Breath, Your Belly, Your Mind

There is a Zen story about a man riding a horse. He seemed to be going somewhere important with great urgency and determination. An observer asked, "Where are you going in such haste?" The man replied: "I don't know. Ask the horse."

Just like that man, who let his horse control his direction and destination instead of consciously controlling his horse, most of us breathe unconsciously. Conscious breathing transforms you into a masterful driver of the chariot called "Life." When you breathe consciously, you are no longer pulled by the wild horse called "your mind." I'm going to show you how you can change your state of mind simply by consciously engaging in specific techniques. Each BE Break will help you take control of the reins of your mind so you can create a supportive environment in your body—especially when you are stressed or anxious.

Breathing is the beginning and ending of your journey as human being! Breathing is where life begins and ends. That is why it is one of the most effective cures for stress and anxiety. Your breath, your belly, and your mind are your ultimate team for success in healing and thriving because your mind and your body take cues from each other. Your breath is the communication bridge between your mind and your emotional state.

**Conscious breathing transforms you
into a masterful driver of the chariot called "Life."**

How you breathe can make you feel better—or worse. Breath and emotion are intimately connected. When your mind sends a message of stress, anxiety, or fear, for example, your breath responds by being rapid, short, and irregular. As noted earlier, the body then releases an excess of adrenaline and cortisol. Luckily, it's a two-way communication. If you slow down your breathing, you slow down the body, and the mind responds by sending a message to the body: *Relax.*

Focused breathing is the most effective way to calm the mind and relieve stress. One of the most powerful aspects of yoga, which offers a scientific method for controlling the breath, stilling the mind, and producing deep relaxation is called *Pranayama*. Prana (Chi) means "vital life force energy." Pranayama not only stills the mind, it enhances your vitality and well-being. This translates into you being more efficient and productive throughout your day. The impact of these techniques on your nervous system and on your overall health is remarkable.

The study of breathing is rooted in ancient philosophy. For centuries, we have been called to examine our breath and how it connects us to our source. Science has recently discovered a neural circuit in our brains that actually responds to our breathing patterns. When we control our breath, it immediately impacts our brains. This neural circuit has been called the "breathing pacemaker" because of its ability to improve and even transform the nervous system's function, all based on our breath.

When your breath is deliberate and controlled, your nervous system's circuitry slows down. Activity decreases. On the other hand, when your breath is erratic or scattered, the circuit responds in kind and its activity increases. Researchers are still uncovering exactly why and how this happens, but simply knowing this pathway exists is a huge step forward in uncovering the secret to health and well-being. Many eastern healing traditions hold that we are born with a pre-destined number of breaths. So, when you slow down your breathing, you are potentially extending your life. It certainly helps to restore your nervous system, which helps your heart, your lungs, your digestion, and on and on.

Breath Affects Memory

Another recent study[1] shows us something interesting. It tells us that the rhythm of your breathing triggers specific electrical activity in your brain, influencing the part of your brain responsible for memory. Going even further, evidence suggests that your mental recall hinges on whether you are breathing through your nose or breathing through your mouth, and whether you are inhaling or exhaling.

In the study, scientists found that when participants were inhaling through their noses, they recalled more fear-based memories. They also found that memory was triggered more often and objects were more easily recalled when participants were inhaling than when they were exhaling.

Researchers believe that when you breathe deeply though your nose, it stimulates a part of the brain's emotional epicenter, releasing memories and emotions. Breathing (particularly inhaling) stimulates the hippocampus (the brain's memory center), which leads to an obvious increase in memories and emotions, and enhances your ability to recall important information when you need it.

---

[1] Systems Neurobiology Laboratory, Department of Neurobiology, David Geffen School of Medicine, University of California. Los Angeles, CA.

Setting Yourself Up for Success: Creating Balance

We are creatures of habit. Our habits help shape our life experience. It's just as easy to have supportive habits as it is to have disempowering ones. It's about what you choose to invest your time and energy in.

There is a Native American story about a troubled young boy who goes to his grandfather for advice. "Grandfather," he says, "I feel as if there are two wolves in my heart fighting for my attention. One is fierce and angry, full of hate. The other is gentle and peaceful, full of love. Which one will win the battle?"

His grandfather answers, "The one you feed."

You may feel that the pull of your non-supportive habits is stronger than your new, supportive habits. Fear has a strong magnetic pull that wants to take over. Peace is neutral, it requires that you choose it. Have you ever noticed how hard it is to resist getting pulled into a gossipy conversation or chiming in to complain about something at work or something political? Just know that the moment-by-moment choices you make—by engaging with your new BE Break habit—will help to create healing space in your body. This can help you to be less vulnerable to the magnetic pull of negativity. Taking BE Breaks is a habit that becomes more magnetic and easier each time you do it. Before long, you will see that the pull of your negative habits lessens day by day.

One of my clients, Jenny, a seventy-one-year-old retired school teacher, had a debilitating habit. She worried excessively. Jenny's habit of jumping into the drama of a situation is a common and deeply ingrained one for many people, but I have to say that we women are particularly good at worrying.

DO-DO RESCUE

Jenny didn't realize that worrying was a habit for her. "It's hard not to worry," she said.

When you resist something, it's always hard because you're in opposition with *what is*.

Usually, it's part of the fear of the unknown and the attachment to the familiar. It takes courage and support to practice engaging with solutions. Drama is addictive. Peace is not. But when you commit to the supportive habit of aligning with the healing opportunity in any situation, over time, it does become easier. After practicing the Do-Be-Do-Be-Do-Be rhythm for a few months, Jenny found that the habit of worrying had less of a grip on her life. "I no longer feel helpless within a situation," she said, smiling.

Jenny had started working with me because of a health crisis. But the healing went far beyond her health. She hadn't realized how much her worry habit had affected her thirty-five-year marriage. Jenny shared with me: "My husband came home from the doctor and I could tell it wasn't great news. Because of my history of overreacting with worry, he didn't want to talk to me about it. I took a quick BE Break and then asked him to talk to me. He was starting to get used to the new, less stressed-out version of me. My voice was calm, we took a breath, and he told me about the alarming results of his blood test. I was able to be there for him without making it worse by panicking and worrying. What would in the past have been a moment of debilitating stress for both of us turned into a loving, bonding experience of support. I was able to be a source of comfort and inspiration as we talked about some of the solutions and I shared some of my BE Break practices with him. Since then, we have both been committed to living a Do-Be-Do-Be-Do-Be life. Thanks to your support, Louise, I know now that it's not about perfection. I still worry. But I don't get stuck there. I'm amazed at how much easier it gets, day by day. I love that my husband is no longer afraid to talk to me about things."

As a mother, I know it's hard not to worry, especially about our loved ones and our children. I think that the most difficult thing, when someone we love is challenged, is not knowing what to do for him or her. We feel helpless. Worrying gives us a socially acceptable thing to do. But when you realize that worrying about someone is like sending a wave of "Yuck," it can help you to change this useless habit. Remember, it takes the same amount of time and energy to send someone good energy, like Light and Love, as it does to send "Yucky" energy. So, instead of calling in more bad energy, take a BE Break. Create the calm in the storm within yourself first.

From that place within you, send out love. Visualize in your mind's eye a pink or green ray of light coming from your heart toward their heart. Take a moment and be in relationship with the healing opportunity for yourself and your loved one(s). From there, you can more easily come up with solutions and attract needed support. Taking a BE Break is one of the most empowering things you can do when you feel scared. It's an empowering way for you to contribute to your higher good—and to the highest good of all.

The Three Keys to Success with Your BE Breaks

Key #1 Positive Thinking

Optimism diffuses stress. It's not so much about going into a happy place as it is about being open to the opportunity to heal a situation or yourself. It's about being willing to let go of the drama within the story and forgive. Forgiving is giving yourself permission to heal. It can start by using a positive thought or affirmation to enhance the results of any of your self-care activities, especially your BE Breaks. But to ensure the healing effectiveness of a positive thought, formulate your affirmations carefully.

Peter was a registrant in one of the corporate stress management programs I presented at his company. He was waiting for the right moment to debunk the idea of positive affirmation. "It doesn't work," he said, making his point enthusiastically. He pulled out a huge stack of papers. "Here it is," he said. "Pages and pages of an affirmation I was working with. I wrote it down hundreds of times, every day. It just does NOT work."

I looked at his pages of beautiful penmanship—line after line of his affirmation. "I see that you are using the phrases "I want" and "I need," I said. "Do you still want and need what you have here?"

"Yes," he said with a "gotcha" tone. "Now more than before I started." "Then it worked." I said.

He sat there like a balloon, slowly deflating.

Be careful about using phrases such as "I want" or "I need" because these indicate lack, and they will only leave you wanting or needing. It is best to use simple, affirmative phrases. I have suggested a few you can use later in this section.

In the early 1900's, Émile Coué, a pharmacist in Nancy, France, had great success healing people with positive thoughts. One of his most famous quotes translates into English as: "Every day in every way, I am getting better and better."

Coué was a thinker who understood the law of manifestation long before it became the stuff of modern pop psychology. His phrase continues to inspire people even today.

My clients have had positive results using variations of this phrase on a daily basis. Positive affirmations have been a big part of my own healing journey as well. Using positive words that align you with *what you do want* (*not* the specific problem facing you) can shift the energy in your mind and in your body. Don't lie to yourself, saying "I feel great," if the subtext is "I feel horrible." Instead, express out loud that your choice is to create the space to allow your body to feel better. In eastern traditions, for example, they use mantras that work similarly to affirmations. I have found using these mantras to be powerful and helpful, to align my mind with my choice to keep my energy up and positive. It also helps to resist the urge to go into "the drama of the story."

The Positive Impact of Sound on Your Brain

I find that the simpler the mantra or affirmation you use, the better. This avoids turning positive thinking into an intellectual exercise. Remember, *a BE Break is about giving your mind a break.* My easy and quick "go-to mantra" is saying the Sanskrit *bij,* or seed words *Sat Nam,* silently. Say *Sat* (meaning *truth*) mentally as you inhale and *Nam* (meaning *name* or *identity*) on your exhale. *Sat Nam* affirms your intention to shift out of the drama to align with your true identity and reconnects you with your inner truth, reminding you that you are not your emotions. For example, if you feel angry, avoid saying "I *am* angry." Instead, state "I *feel* angry and I choose to bring healing to this situation." Or, you can say, "I am Truth, I am Light, I am Peace." These phrases can work well in the moment. Sat Nam has a natural connection to the sound and rhythm of your heartbeat, so it is a great tool for both positive thinking and concentration.

The extended form of Sat Nam is Sa-Ta-Na-Ma. I use this mantra throughout my day with my BE Breaks any time I feel anxious and need to clean out my mind. It's often referred to as the "garbage truck" as it does a great job at interrupting and clearing both conscious and sub-conscious negative thoughts.

I learned these mantras early on in my Kundalini yoga practice. I have found them to be great to shift my brain and my body into a more positive vibration. It might help you to understand why these sounds work if I explain some of their physiological effects on your mind and body. Notice that the primal sounds Ssss, Tttt, Nnnn, and Mmmm, together with Aaaaa, create "Sa-Ta-Na-Ma." Each of these consonants engages the tip of the tongue to the upper palate and the lips. The Mmmm creates a vibration in the bones of your skull where the pituitary and pineal glands are located. The Mmmm also create vibrations on the lips, affecting some crucial acupressure points around the lips. Yuri Danilov, a Senior Scientist at the University of Wisconsin-Madison, led a study about the healing effects of the tip of the tongue (to enhance the healing process for MS patients). In an article in *Scientific American*, Esther Hsieh reports Danilov stating that, "The tongue has extensive motor and sensory integration with the brain. The nerves on the tip of the tongue are directly connected to the brain stem, a crucial hub that directs basic bodily processes." In both my Kundalini and Chi Gong training, I also learned that connecting the tip of the tongue to the upper palate creates a circuit for energy (prana or chi) to move through specific organs and glands to enhance the benefits for specific exercises.

So, after saying "Sa-Ta-Na-Mmmmm" ... we add the Aaaaa sound. Take a breath right now and exhale: "Aaaahhhhhh." Can you feel the immediate relaxing impact it has? Aaaahhhhh moves the energy through an open mouth to release tension. I use the naturally healing "Aaaa" sound throughout my JoyFull Yoga and Sound Healing classes; it always gets me and my students into a sweet, open, and relaxed state of mind and body.

I go into more depth about the impact of healing sounds on the body and mind in my upcoming book, *The Missing Peace*. I wanted to introduce and demystify the Sa-Ta-Na-Ma mantra to you in this book because it has been one of the most helpful parts of my BE Breaks. You can use Sa-Ta-Na-Ma with any of the BE Breaks—I find it more beneficial than counting "one, two, three, four." I encourage you to try it and see (or feel) for yourself.

I also like the simplicity of both "Sat Nam" and the "Sa-Ta-Na-Ma" form. In Sanskrit, the form is called Gurumukhi. Gurumukhi is a language writing system used in the sacred texts of the Sikh tradition; it means "from the mouth of the teacher." Sa-Ta-Na-Ma translates in English as:

Sa = Infinity, cosmos, beginning.

Ta = Life, existence.

Na = Completion, rest, the end.

Ma = Rebirth, transformation.

It's not always easy to reach for a positive thought when we are in crisis. For example, I remember the time I got pickpocketed. I had just returned home from a business trip to L.A. when I got a call from one of my friends from my recovery group who was in need of support. I suggested we

Do-Do Rescue

meet at a support meeting around the corner. I grabbed my wallet, stuck it in my coat pocket, and went out the door.

It was a crowded meeting and I hung my coat over the back of my chair. I was tired and a bit jet lagged. As we were leaving, I put my coat on and slipped my hands in my coat pockets and ... my wallet, with all my cash and all my important cards, was gone. I was so upset. I got home and made calls to cancel my credit cards. Then I remembered my driver's license and the other important documentation that was still in my wallet from my recent travel. There was nothing I could do about it. I felt sick with anxiety. All I could do was say over and over, "Let there be LIGHT."

That night, I went to bed repeating this phrase, along with the Sa-Ta-Na-Ma, over and over, to keep the poison of fear out of my body. At 1:00 a.m., I heard the buzzing of the intercom. I had barely fallen asleep. I got up to answer the intercom and the doorman told me, "There's a smelly guy at the door with your wallet. He wants money or booze in exchange for your wallet."

"I don't have money or booze," I replied.

When the doorman conveyed my message to the man at the door, the man walked out of the building.

"Let there be Light, Let there be Light," I said, as I hung up the intercom. "Sa-Ta-Na-Ma" ...

I kept repeating it to get my mind and body to calm down.

The doorman called me back a few minutes later. "The guy came back and threw your wallet into the lobby."

I got dressed and ran downstairs. All my important ID cards were there! I was so relieved. If you have ever had to go to New York City's DMV office for a new driver's license, you know what a gift it was to get it back.

Bringing Light into a dark situation will always help you create and attract a solution.

Remember, it's much easier to find your way out of a dark moment with the light on!

Affirmations You Can Use Regularly:

- I align with my Higher good and the Higher good of all.
- In this moment now, I choose to breathe Peace into every cell of my body.
- In this moment now, I choose to breathe healing Light into every cell of my body.
- In this moment now, I choose to breathe Love into every cell of my body.
- Every day, in every way, I am open to the healing opportunity to restore radiant health in my body, in my mind, and in my spirit.
- I release all that is not serving my well-being now and I call in all that supports me and my Higher good now.
- I align with peaceful resolutions in all areas of my life.
- I lovingly accept and appreciate who I am as I am now.

Key #2 Concentration

The mind is like a monkey, jumping, interacting with, and responding to all external stimuli. In times of stress, I have experienced that I have a hard time staying focused. I discovered some time ago that I possess traits of Attention Deficit Disorder (ADD). My monkey mind is particularly hard to contain. I think that is why I have been able to help so many busy people who claim they can't meditate. For example, my client, Joseph, claimed to have an untamable active mind.

Joseph had worked his way up to the position of vice-president in his company. At age fifty-five, he was at the top of his game—and on the verge of a heart attack. He knew he needed the Do-Do Rescue remedy. He was ready to make some major lifestyle changes, and they included my Do-Be-Do-Be-Do-Be program. "I don't know that I can do it," Joseph told me, "because I can't shut my mind off."

**The truth is, you can't shut your mind down.
You need to redirect it.**

The truth is, you can't shut your mind down. You need to redirect it. Learning how to support your mind with concentration is all it takes to get started. Below are two simple ways to enhance your concentration on-the-spot. You can use what works best for you to help you refocus your mind. You can make the two options below a part of any of the BE Breaks found in Chapter 4. As you do these exercises, observe what happens to your body. You won't be able to resist becoming calmer. Notice that as your breathing naturally slows down, it causes your heart rate to slow down. Inner peace begins.

Focus to Still Your Active Mind

Option 1: Eyes closed gently: The simple act of gently closing your eyes is by far the best way to shut off outside stimuli. When doing this first exercise, center your attention at the root of your nose (the point between your eyebrows). Closing your eyes creates deeper concentration and triggers neuroendocrine balancing.

Option 2: Eyes open: This was Joseph's biggest *aha*. He had a hard time closing his eyes. When practicing a BE Break, you may find yourself in a situation in which you can't close your eyes. Choose an object or image to focus on that has a "feel good" or neutral quality for you (e.g. a flower, a favorite pen, or a picture of the beach). Be careful using pictures of your children, though. If you've had "one of those mornings," gazing at family photos may not induce a feeling of relaxation. Try this easy, anytime-anywhere solution: Simply clasp your hands together with fingers conjoined, thumbs pointed upward, with thumb pads pressed together. Then, focus on the "V" shape where your thumbs meet.

Another group of power tools for concentration are symbolic hand gestures called Mudras. These are hand positions that involve connecting your fingers in a specific way to help create energy seals that relate to your Mind-Body system. I talk more about this in Chapter 4. For example, bring your thumb and your index finger together so they are touching lightly. Think of your thumb as representing you *doing* (your body) and your index finger representing *you being* (your peaceful mind). This simple hand gesture, called

"Gyan Mudra," can be a supportive trigger for your intention to bring your body and mind into harmony with each other.

When I learned about acupuncture points, it made sense to me why and how mudras can be so powerful. In acupuncture, the channels responsible for your energy that flow throughout your body are called *meridians*. All your acupuncture points begin or end at your hands and feet. Your hands in general are part of the heart meridian and we know that the heart leads the orchestra that helps our body to stay alive. So, it makes sense to me that using the tips of your fingers to stimulate other meridians can impact the well-being of your whole body. On a more practical note, your body learns *triggers*. If, for example, you use a certain hand gesture every time you want to calm your body and concentrate, your body and your mind will remember that cue. Later, you'll have many opportunities to practice different hand gestures (mudras) with some of your BE Breaks. I always encourage you to try and feel for yourself if using a mudra helps you to improve your concentration.

Practicing Key #1 and Key #2: Sound and Mudra:

Here is an easy and effective way to help you clear your mind from negativity and stress. As it helps to improve brain function, it allows you to practice staying focused and in the moment. It uses the bij or seed sounds of Sa - Ta - Na - Ma. These vibrations create a current that has been documented to clear and balance the right and left hemispheres of the brain. In their book, *Meditation as Medicine*, authors, Dr. Dharma Singh Khalsa and Cameron Stauth, share some of their case studies that show the many benefits of this particular mantra meditation, called Kirtan Kriya (mentioned above), used in Kundalini Yoga.

Dr. Dharma Singh compares the impact of the tongue striking the upper palate as you make these sounds to the impact of striking the keys on a computer, referring to the computer as the mind.

Sitting comfortably, rest your hands facing upwards, in your lap. Close your eyes and focus at the point between your eyebrows.

- As you say: Sa ... touch your index finger to your thumb.
    Ta ... touch your middle finger to your thumb.
    Na ... touch your ring finger to your thumb.
    Ma ... touch your pinkie finger to your thumb.
- Repeat, starting again with your index finger.
    - For the first two minutes, use your full voice, then...
    - For two minutes, say the mantra in a whisper, then...
    - For four minutes, say the mantra silently (Say Sa-Ta-Na-Ma in your head).
- Then, reverse the order:
    - Say the mantra for two minutes in a whisper, then,

- End with two minutes in full voice.

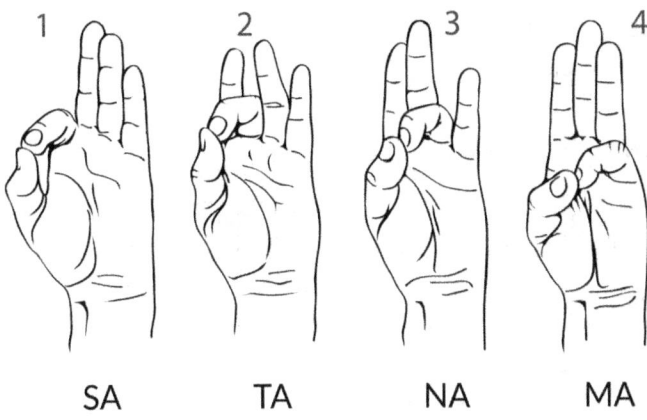

SA　TA　NA　MA

You can use this practice anytime to help you with concentration and anxiety and improve your overall cognitive function. The studies on its benefits for improving memory have gained the attention of the Alzheimer's Research and Prevention Foundation. They also recommend twelve minutes a day. I often use it as a BE Break on the spot when I'm in a stressful situation, by repeating the sounds mentally ... I do the fingering with my hands in my pockets. For me, it works every time at calming my mind.

Key #3: Continuity

The more you do something, the easier it gets. But it only works if you *do it*—and no one can do it for you. For example, a gym membership isn't going to have an impact on your fitness level on its own. Results require your participation.

Understand that a habit, good or bad, is a subconscious chain reaction that takes place between the mind, the glandular system, and the nervous system. Giving up being stressed-out may cause certain physical and emotional symptoms of withdrawal—much like giving up coffee or sugar does. Of course, you may have developed some of your disempowering habits at a very young age (I did) and those can take a bit longer to release.

Identifying Unsupportive Habits:

Unsupportive habits are the things you do automatically that do not make you feel good. Is there anything you are doing that is impacting your health right now? That's an unsupportive habit. For example, a client of mine, Jarred, had a habit of getting up in the morning and drinking up to three cups of coffee as he jumped into reading his clients' emails. Changing that kind of unsupportive habit needs to go at the top of your list. Other unsupportive habits, like worrying, can impact your relationships. (Later, I'll share a story about that.) As you read this book, make a list of the habits you have that pull you out of feeling good. At the end of the book, you can prioritize them, starting with the ones that have the greatest negative impact on your health and well-being. As you've noticed, I keep stressing throughout this book the importance of setting yourself realistic, achievable goals. The important thing is to replace unsupportive habits with supportive ones. Then, you need to commit to developing and nurturing your new, supportive habits. When it feels challenging, remember, you're just steps away from forming new, supportive habits and living your Do-Be-Do-Be-Do-Be lifestyle!

Choosing Supportive Habits to Commit to:

A supportive habit is one that you feel serves your Higher good in a way that respects your limitations and the reality of your current lifestyle. In other words, establishing realistic and sustainable goals is the key to long-term change and success. If making time to calm your body and mind is new for you, start with being consistent with three to ten minutes a day for forty to ninety days and build from there. I suggest you make a list of three to five new supportive habits you would like to bring into your life now. You will have lots to choose from when you get done reading this book.

To establish your Do-Be-Do-Be-Do-Be rhythm, I suggest you start with at least three BE Breaks (see Chapter 4) and commit to doing them for forty consecutive days. Mark your calendar!

At intervals over the next forty days, evaluate how it is going for you. Note the benefits you are reaping. In forty days, you will rewire that chain reaction and your BE Breaks will become deeply ingrained, supportive habits that support your goals. Make adjustments ... maybe even increase the duration of one of your BE Breaks. If it's going well, perhaps add two more BE Breaks and keep going for another fifty days—so that BE Breaks become second nature.

To help you become consistent at taking your BE Breaks, it's important to schedule specific times to practice. Write your BE Breaks in your calendar, set your phone to alert you when it's time to take a BE Break, or use stick-on notes in appropriate places to prompt yourself to remember to take your BE Break. If you have a change in your schedule that prevents you from doing a scheduled practice, reschedule it, just as you would an important appointment. The habit of making time and making your well-being important to you will also nurture your self-worth and help you to stay committed to your practice of self-care.

Continual practice will strengthen your positive habits and make them easier for you to recall when you need them on the spot or in times of crisis. The more you practice, the more benefits you will reap—and the more you'll be sure to avoid overwhelm or burnout.

Practicing the Three Keys:

You can use the following affirmation prayer to practice integrating the Three Keys. The detailed visualization helps your mind stay engaged so you can practice both positive thinking and concentration. It has an instant "feel good effect" that can keep you motivated to do it daily to practice continuity. It's one of my favorite ways to shift out of a challenging and stressful mindset.

Sunlight ~ Divine Light & Peace Prayer

Before you start, take a few slow, gentle breaths:

Close your eyes and visualize a sun rising in your mind's eye.

Imagine sitting in sunlight at the horizon where the sky and earth meet. See yourself in Sun Light (Divine Light). Let it surround you.

As you say the words below, imagine drawing a diamond shape around you.

> "Light at my left, Light behind me, Light at my right, and Light in front of me, Light all around me."

Then, visualize drawing another diamond shape, large enough to surround you.

> "Light above me, Light behind me, Light below me, Light in front of me, Light surrounds me."

See yourself basking in this healing Sun Light ~ Divine Light.

Do-Do Rescue

See yourself in the center of a 3-D diamond shape.
   "Light into every cell of my body now."

Take a gentle breath in. ~ Pause. ~ As you exhale, say...
   "I release any negative energy."

Repeat one or two more times as needed.
   "I send out Light to all the situations in my life.
   I send out Light to all the people in my life.
   I send out Light to ALL,
   Light to the Universe.
   Thank you."

If you have more time, continue.

Bring in the intention of Peace with each breath now.
  "I light a candle of Peace in front of me.
  I light a candle of Peace behind me.
  I light a candle of Peace to my left.
  And a candle of Peace to my right.
  Peace surrounds me.
  I invite Peace in every cell of my body now."

Take a gentle breath in. ~ Pause. ~ As you exhale, say:
  "I release any negative thoughts.
  I call in peaceful resolutions into all the situations in my life now.
  I send out Peace to all the people in my life.
  I send out Peace to All.
  Peace to the Universe.
  Thank you."

Place your left hand on the center of your chest and your right hand on top of your left.
  "I now invite the unconditional Love of the Divine to surround me."

Mentally draw a diamond shape with each intention.
  "Love to my left, Love behind me, Love to my right, Love in front of me.
  I call in Love all around me now as I claim my place of inner harmony between sky and earth.
  I breathe Love into every cell of my body now."

Take a gentle breath in. ~ Pause. ~ Exhale.
  "I send out love to all the people in my life. I send out Love to ALL,
  Love to the Universe.
  Thank you."

I strongly recommend that you use this prayer daily and any time fear and worry are trying to take you down a dark alley of negativity. (You can access a recorded version at www.DoDoRescue.com)

CHAPTER 4
THE DO-DO
RESCUE REMEDY

The solution to overwhelm—and the way to avoid it altogether—is to manage your stress levels throughout your day. That's where BE Breaks come in. Each BE Break gives you techniques and strategies to lower your stress levels and helps you align with choices that support your overall well-being and create more balance in your body and in your life. By taking these strategic breaks, you can enjoy more energy and less pain and fatigue in your body, mind, and spirit.

The "Three Life-Saving Breaths"

"Just take a deep breath and you'll be fine." We hear this classic advice often, and we know that it is rooted in profound truth. As I noted earlier, how you take in a deep breath is crucial. With the "Three Life-Saving Breaths" practice, I am talking about committing to taking three full yogic breaths—meaning that you take the time to connect and concentrate on your breath a minimum of three times in your day. Make a commitment to yourself to take three non-negotiable BE Breaks that consist of a minimum of three intentional, slow breaths. This is a realistic and "doable" commitment that can get you off the "I forgot" path to failure. The impact of staying committed can be profound.

So, let's start by establishing what a "deep breath" is. When I'm giving a talk, there may be hundreds or even thousands of people in the room. When I say, "Take a deep breath," I see an ocean of shoulders go up. A deep breath is often misunderstood—most people pull their bellies up as they breathe in, which actually makes it impossible for the lungs to fill up completely ... there's no room left. Learning to take a full, deep breath with the belly relaxed and stretched out is part of learning to create healing space and balance in your body.

To create balance in your life, you need to create balance in your day. To have balance in your day, you need to create balance in your body. There is no better place to start than by tapping into the crucial part of being alive—your breath. No matter what situation you find yourself in, you have to breathe. Using something you have to do anyway as a tool to improve your well-being is smart and sustainable. Breathing is a crucial part—and indeed, the ultimate part—of an on-the-spot Do-Do Rescue and Stress Relief Remedy. Connecting to your breath and mindfully carving out the time to do so will impact every area of your life.

**No matter what situation you find yourself in, you have to breathe.
Breathing is the ultimate on-the-spot Do-Do Rescue Remedy.**

The Full Yogic Breath – Breathing as an Action

This is where it all begins! To practice a full yogic breath, start by putting one hand, palm down, on your abdomen. Place the other hand in the center of your chest. Now, think about softening the belly. Relax your shoulders and your chest. As you breathe, inhale through your nose. Feel your belly expanding, then feel your chest expanding. Be sure to keep your shoulders down. As you exhale through your nose, be mindful not to collapse. Think of lengthening your body as you pull your navel in, expelling all the air from your lungs.

Most of us usually do not breathe fully, so it may take a little practice. Most people take in shallow, rapid breaths and bring air only into the upper part of their lungs. (If you are having difficulty bringing in enough breath to expand your abdomen, try lying down and crossing your arms over your chest. This will force the in-breath to fill the lower part of your lungs.)

The full yogic breath allows your body to take in more oxygen as you fill your belly and chest and expand your clavicle. As you pull the navel in on your exhale, you get rid of all the stale air so you can invite more oxygen to come into your lungs on your next in-breath.

The Power of a Conscious Breath – Breathing Like You Mean It

We are constantly communicating our intentions to the Universe with our thoughts, mostly unconsciously. We take breathing for granted. The mind is left to ruminate on random thoughts as we go from one to-do to another. Your breath is one of the ongoing sources of support for your body; it orchestrates the flow of your life force. Every breath you take tells the story of how you are choosing to engage with your life force. When you are in charge of your thoughts and aware of your life-supporting breath, you can ignite the power of your intention to create a supportive, healing environment for your body and your life. When you are taking your BE Breaks, be sure to breathe like you mean it! Each breath is a great way for you to practice opening your whole self, to receive and let go completely, to release tension through your exhale.

Overall Benefits

The moment you choose to take a full, deep breath, you immediately reduce hormonal overload. Your heart rate settles, your blood pressure stabilizes. This creates a chain reaction that helps to moderate your adrenaline and cortisol levels. When you connect to your life force, you enter into a partnership with your body. It allows you to take back the power of your mind so you can clearly assess every situation and see things with a different spin.

Strategies for Using the Full

Yogic Breath Technique

If you only practice calming exercises "when you think of it" you are not going to be consistent and will not reap the full benefit of your BE Breaks.

- Commit to taking three mindful "yogic" breaths, three times a day.
- Choose three different intervals: one in the morning, one at midday, and one in the evening.
- Set a reminder in your phone, write it down on your schedule, or leave a sticky note anywhere you'll see it.
- Stop what you are doing. Saying the word "Release" three times can help you to let go of what you are doing and be more focused on your BE Break.

- Connect with your breath by placing one hand on your belly and, if possible, put the other hand on the center of your chest.
- Doing a yogic breath is a great way to start and end your day, so think about your breath at bedtime and again when you wake up in the morning.
- Throughout your day, if you're faced with anxiety or stress, simply *pause*. Connect with your breathing for three conscious breaths. Tap into your intention to receive some ease and to release the tension in your body. Let gravity help you to let go.
- Prior to engaging in any physical activity (from walking to working out), set your intention and take three deep breaths before you start. This will help you slow down the pace and allow you to get much more out of your workout.
- Every day, schedule a BE Break with the intention of becoming aware and breathing fully and slowly for no less than one to three uninterrupted minutes. Remember, this is a productive time for you to invest in your health-care.
- Put your phone on "Do Not Disturb" mode, set a timer, and gift yourself with your own undivided attention. This could be before you get out of your car when you arrive at work in the morning, on your lunch break, or at home. It's also perfect if you have a train or bus commute. You can include the finger holding exercises in BE Break: Hands-On (p. 104-105) to enhance your relaxation and well-being.
- While connecting with your breath, come into a mindset of gratitude. Dwelling in gratitude while connecting with your breath is a beautiful way to expand your practice.

BE Break

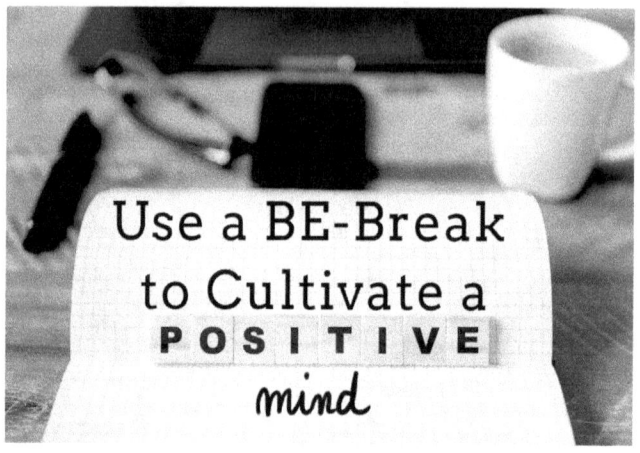

BE Break: Mind-Full Breathing to Calm Your Mind and Body:

Breathe in through your nose to the count of eight (building up to the count of twenty), and out through your nose for the same count.

Feel how, as your breath slows down, your whole body becomes calm.

This is the beginning of conscious breathing; it allows you to regain control of your mind. By doing this for at least three breaths, you allow your body to restore itself as you begin to feel more and more relaxed. (Note: Count to eight at a slow and steady rate. It sometimes helps to count "1 and 2 and 3 and 4, etc.")

BE Break: The Three Life-Saving Breaths

- Relax your shoulders by pressing them slightly back and then down as you straighten your spine.

- Start with one hand on your belly, and the other on the center of your chest.

- Relax and soften your belly and chest. Feel your belly and chest expanding as you inhale.

- Then, on the exhale, engage your belly and draw it inward, toward your spine.

- Inhale for the count of eight; exhale for the count of eight. (Breathe to the count of four if eight is too much.) Work gradually up to the count of twenty.

- Say your affirmation mentally as you inhale. As you exhale, say the word "Release," mentally or out loud.

- Repeat this three times.

Feel the breath coming into your belly and chest

Other Ways to Practice Your "Three Life-Saving Breaths"

There are a multitude of breathing techniques. I'm sharing a few of my favorites in this book that are effective and easy to use on the spot. Specifically, for the "Three Life-Saving Breaths," I recommend you use specific ratios of counts to regulate the flow of your breathing. You'll notice a variation in the ratios of the counts. It may help you to know that your inhalation stimulates your sympathetic nervous system, and your exhalation stimulates the parasympathetic nervous system. That is why, when you are gearing up to do something physical, your body tends to take more air in than it lets out, to activate the sympathetic nervous system, which increases your heart rate to get you physically ready for action. When you are agitated, your body is focused on taking in more air to get ready to fight or flee. Your parasympathetic system does the opposite. It activates relaxation in your body and lowers your blood pressure. A 1:1 ratio breathing pattern attempts to get the two systems to work together in harmony in your mind and body. When you are particularly anxious and agitated, a few breaths with a longer exhalation can help deactivate the overactive sympathetic nervous system to help you calm down. Counting your breaths in and out is in itself an effective way to engage the mind immediately and begin to lower your blood pressure and the overall stress level in your body. You may find yourself needing to count faster at first, but as you practice, your lung capacity will improve and it will become easier for you to slow the breath down more and more. The ratio is the important thing to pay attention to. In addition to the above balancing 1:1 ratio, or eight count in – eight count out, below are a few other ways you can practice the "Three Life-Saving Breaths."

BE Break

BE Break: The 4-7-8 Breath

If you are feeling particularly anxious or agitated, making the breath out longer than the breath in will activate the parasympathetic system to create an immediate calming effect. It will also help you release anxiety from your body and reduce tension within three to four breaths.

- Breathe in through your nose for four counts.

- Hold the breath in for the count of seven, also allowing the body to expand and relax.

- Exhale powerfully through the mouth, making a "Tchhhewwwoooohhh" sound through the rounded lips for eight counts or until your lungs feel empty.

- Repeat only three to four times.

Be Break: The 8-4-8-4 Breathing Ratio

- In this variation, you suspend the breath in and out. You may notice that holding your breath out can be more challenging than holding the breath in. It can bring up fear. If it does, think about releasing the fear and mentally remind yourself: "All is well." Be gentle, don't force it. You can start with holding your breath out for just a moment. Over time, you can slow down the rate of your counts as you are able. Doing the 4-7-8 ratio a few times before doing this 8-4-8-4 breath can help facilitate your practice.

- Breathe through your nose as you expand your belly for the count of eight.

- Hold your breath for the count of four as you allow your body to create space and relaxation.

- Let the tension out of your body as you let the breath go, exhaling through your nose for the same count. Then, if you can, be still ... hold your breath out for the count of four.

Be Break: The 8-4-8-4 Breathing Ratio

- *Practice this at least three times.* To truly reap the full benefits, do it for one to three minutes.

- You can also try doing this technique with your hands interlaced behind your head, to release tension in your chest and open the lungs more deeply. Once this ratio is easy for you, you can do a more advanced version: the 8-8-8-4 ratio. You do it the same way, only you hold the breath in for eight counts instead of four.

These are powerful, self-healing BE Break techniques to de-stress and relax your body and mind and to help you to diffuse anxiety and fear anytime you need to. Again, don't forget about continuity. The more you practice, the easier it gets—and the more benefits you will reap!

"Tension is who you think you should be,
Relaxation is who you are."
~ Chinese proverb

THE POWER OF YOUR HANDS FOR SELF-HEALING

One of my New York City clients, Jane, was extremely skeptical about the idea of BE Breaks, but she was desperate to try anything for her debilitating anxiety—and she had seen remarkable changes in a friend who had been working with me. Jane had tried repeatedly to take her entrance exam to get into her desired psychology program but her anxiety got the best of her each time. She tried taking BE Breaks and was amazed at how effective they were; she loved that she could use them on the spot. Well, Jane passed her exam and her new way of navigating her day with the Do-Be-Do-Be-Do-Be rhythm helped improve her relationship with her teenage son. She told me: "I'm not coming from my stressed-out self all the time. When I take a BE Break, I can meet my son from a calm, less reactive place and we can actually talk to each other instead of getting into a screaming match all the time. He's commented that the BE Break thing is weird but also "cool." The other day I saw him in his room doing his own BE Break himself. I couldn't believe it. He's right. It's super cool."

So, remember, whatever challenges you might have in your life, BE Breaks will help you meet and overcome them more efficiently—and they'll help to prevent you from over-reacting and escalating a problem. The benefits will affect other parts of your life positively as well. You can give yourself a hand to shift out of the Do-Do into Do-Be-Do-Be-Do-Be—literally. In yoga, we use our hands to enhance healing opportunities. In Chinese medicine and acupuncture, hands and feet are the beginnings and ends of the roadmaps for energy to move throughout the body. As noted earlier, these pathways are called *meridians*. You can't see them the way you see veins running through your body beneath your skin, but in Eastern healing modalities meridians are mapped out as reference points. A lot of this makes sense to me. For example, your hands are part of the heart meridian. If you draw a line up your arms from your hands, you end up at the heart. The ancient science behind this concept is more complex than that but, what I know is that it works. I encourage you to be curious—try the suggested hand gestures below with your BE Breaks and see (and feel it) for yourself.

I want to give you a brief introduction to the power of your hands so you can understand why we use certain fingers and hand gestures (or "mudras") to enhance some of the "BE" practices. I received my information about the healing power of hands from Traditional Chinese medicine teachings, as well as through my studies of the Ayurveda approach to healing.

Your Emotions in the Palms of Your Hands

In Chinese and Ayurvedic medicine, practitioners talk about the influence your emotions have on the flow of the energy in your body, which they say impacts your physical state of well-being. It makes sense, doesn't it? When you feel bad emotionally, it's hard to feel good in your body. The drama of a stressful situation can trigger emotions. That's when we let go of the steering wheel and let fear take over. The chain reaction begins. Emotions create tension in the body; the breath becomes shallow or rapid and immediately interrupts the healthy flow of your life force. To reclaim a harmonious, healthy flow of energy in your physical body, you need to balance your emotions and mind. When you feel upset, angry, fearful, sad, frustrated, etc., negative energy moves throughout your body. Just like negative thoughts, when these dense feelings stay in your body for an extended period, they compromise your immune system and the body can start to break down. Have you ever noticed how often you catch a cold when you go through a rough patch in life or when you are overworked?

Positive emotions also impact the body. Laughter, for example, helps produce endorphins, your body's natural feel-good chemicals. Positive emotions help boost your immune system and make it easier for you to make supportive decisions. When you get stuck in the stress of emotions and keep on *doing*, you become less productive. Taking BE Breaks to cultivate a more harmonious emotional state can give you an extra boost during stressful, busy periods and can make you more productive. As I explained earlier, the breath acts as a bridge, and your hands are like the vessel that can help carry you from an emotional upset to a more peaceful state.

Just like your breath, your hands can be used during your BE Breaks to release blocked energy and create a more stable and healing environment in your mind and body. You will notice some mudras included as part of many of the BE Breaks.

Traditional Chinese Medicine (TCM) and Ayurveda reveal that the state of our emotions can affect specific organs. For example: Anger relates to the liver; joy and love impact the heart; sadness has a big impact on the lungs and the heart. Worry impacts the lungs and the spleen; emotions tied to fear have an impact on the kidneys; getting sudden bad news or experiencing a shock will affect the heart. For things to flow we need a clear path, and emotions are like road blocks that restrict the healthy flow of energy between the various systems of the body. All of our energy goes to dealing with the road blocks. Have you ever noticed, for example, that when you are upset, you forget to breathe? This blocks the healthy flow of "prana" or "life force" and your body can't do its job of keeping you healthy. As you shift into a "Do-Be-Do-Be-

Do-Be" rhythm, you give your body a helpline to remember to breathe. By doing this you reclaim your energy and restore the flow of your life force to create a healing environment for your body to do its job more efficiently.

Balancing and Healing Your Whole Self, One Finger at a Time

In the teachings of Kundalini Yoga, Universal Kabbalah, Reflexology, and Chinese and Ayurvedic medicine, I learned many different techniques and theories about the healing power of your hands and feet. There are interesting crossovers between these modalities, all of which indicate that you can balance the energy and emotions in the body through different pressure points found in the hands and feet. It was hard for me to believe at first that something as simple as holding one finger at a time in a particular sequence or positioning my hands in a particular gesture (mudra) with breathing could do so much good. Using mudras works for me and for many of my clients and I encourage you to try the suggested hand gestures with the BE Breaks to discover for yourself the power of your hands. The simple and effective technique below is one of my favorites. I use this especially when I travel and can't do some of the more complex practices. I also like to recommend this as a starting point because it can help you to deepen and heal your relationship with your body and your feelings.

Here is an easy, on-the-spot BE Break to enhance the use of gentle breathing to balance the emotions. I love that you can do this anywhere, at any time. It is a discreet way of taking care of yourself at work, on the bus, train, or plane, etc.

BE Break

BE Break: Hands-On

- Sit comfortably and relax your shoulders by rolling them back three times, then forward three times. Shake your hands lightly at the wrists to release tension.

- Rest your hands in your lap and breathe gently and deeply by relaxing your belly.

- Start by wrapping your right hand around your left thumb. Once you feel a pulsation, or after two to three minutes, switch hands, with your left hand holding your right thumb for the same duration.

- Bring in the intention of kindness as you move slowly from one finger to the next, alternating sides for each finger. You may not feel as much of a pulse in your other fingers as you feel in your thumb. Give yourself a time goal of a minimum of two minutes, or longer as needed.

Practice slowing down your breathing, relaxing the belly as you focus on each finger.

Give each finger your full attention.

Observe what you are feeling.

Allow your thoughts and feelings to arise, but do not engage with them ... let them move on by like clouds in the sky.

Resist the urge to jump into the drama of your feelings by saying the word "RELEASE." Say it three times on your exhale until each thought or feeling passes: "RELEASE. RELEASE. RELEASE." Or, say, "I choose to release and heal _____ *(fill in the emotion or situation) in this moment."*

You can create a deeper state of relaxation by using a sound to help you redirect your mind. I like using the sound of "Sat" (which means "truth" in Sanskrit), mentally on the in-breath, and on the out-breath, using the sound "Nam," (meaning "name or identity"). (So, "Sat Nam" means "My True Identity, My True Essence," or "I choose in this moment to align with My Truth," or "My True-Self"). This technique has proven to be a very effective and easy way of coordinating mind and breath for my clients (and for me).

This entire practice can take about ten to fifteen minutes. If you are short on time and want to focus on one emotion for a specific situation, you can hold the finger that relates to how you are feeling (see below) and do the exercise only on that finger (on both hands) until you feel more peaceful and balanced. In my Universal Kabbalah studies, I learned that each finger is associated with a specific planetary influence. For the purpose of this technique, I want to focus on the information from Chinese medicine, in which each finger relates to different emotions and organs:

The Thumb:

The thumb is sometimes said to relate to the planet Mars, because it holds the element of fire. This is the action planet. In Western cultures, we often give the "okay" for an action with a "thumbs up." The thumb represents the self or the ego. Holding your thumb can be a great way to reclaim your sense of self. The thumb relates to worry, which often can be triggered by fear of the unknown. To ease feelings of worry, depression, and nervousness, hold your thumb. Holding your thumb can also help with digestion as it relates to the meridian for the stomach, spleen, and skin. It can sometimes even help to relieve headaches.

Index Finger:

Your index finger relates to the properties of the planet Jupiter, which represents expansion, growth, and abundance. It is connected to the muscular system, the kidney, and the bladder. To alleviate fear and anxiety, to ease negative self-talk, and to restore your connection to joy and expansion, hold your index finger. When you feel stuck, holding the index finger can support you to see beyond the limits of what you think is possible. According to Chinese medicine, holding the index finger has been known to help relieve muscle cramps, back pain, toothaches, and digestive tract problems.

Middle Finger:

Your middle finger is connected to the planet Saturn—sometimes referred to as "the task master." The middle finger is about "doing the work," taking supportive action to overcome obstacles ... it shows us lessons to be learned. When you want to ease anger, irritability and/or frustrations, hold your middle finger. It will help to reconnect you to feelings of acceptance and compassion. In Traditional Chinese Medicine, the middle finger relates to the blood's circulatory system, the liver, and the gall bladder.

Ring Finger:

Your ring finger relates to the Sun, your vitality, and your radiance. It's the finger that is most likely to shine with jewelry. Hold your ring finger to ease sadness and grief, to bring harmony to the lungs and digestive organs, and to support you in easing feelings of resistance.

Little Finger:

The little finger is connected to the planet Mercury, which relates to communication. Holding your little finger can support you to alleviate anxiety and nurture the feeling of peace in your heart. It can also reduce tension and support the throat and the bones. Massage your little finger to help you improve communication, let go of judgments, and restore self-confidence.

Here is a chart to show you which finger to hold for a specific emotional state.

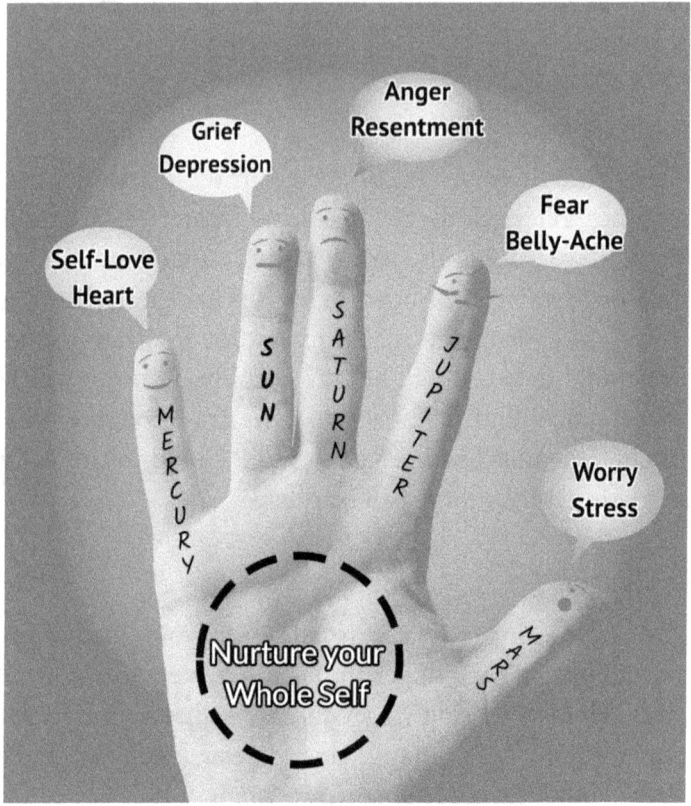

This practice of holding one finger at a time is a powerful way to balance your organ functions and emotions. (I have had acupuncture massage rings made to help with this practice. You can purchase an acupuncture massage ring at www.picosworldwide.com)

You can make this self-healing BE Break part of your daily self-care practice. Try committing to forty consecutive days and before long, you will feel an improvement in your overall well-being.

Why Forty Days?

Forty days is the length of time it takes for a good habit to stick. This number shows up throughout world religions: Jesus spent forty days in the desert; there are forty days of Lent; Muhammad was forty when he received the revelation of the Archangel Gabriel; in the Hebrew Bible story of Noah, the rain fell for forty days and forty nights; Moses was on Mt. Sinai for forty days; in Kabbalah, forty represents the four sides of the earth, etc. The significance of the number forty also came up in my Kundalini yoga training. I've personally experienced the challenge and the power of a forty-day commitment with a practice. As a wellness coach, I've witnessed time and time again in my clients' experience the lasting impact of a forty-day practice. For many, it is one of the turning points in creating lasting transformation. It also provides you with a goal to stay committed and relates to the third key of success: *continuity*.

The more you do a practice, the more powerful it becomes.

Here is another simple relaxation technique that you can use when you are having a busy, stressful day. You can do it anywhere—at the bus stop, in a café, even in the bathroom!

BE Break

Louise Lavergne

BE Break: Hands and Knees

When you don't know what to do, BE ... more present, more peaceful, less agitated.

Sit down and rub your knees.

Breathe as gently and as slowly as you can.

As you rub your knees, say: "In this moment, as I rub my knees, I'm okay. I take a few breaths to reclaim my mind." Ask yourself, "What is the next supportive step I can take in this situation, at this moment?"

As you rub your knees, you are using the bones of your knees to massage the centers of your hands, which have a direct impact on your heart. Metaphysically speaking, your knees represent your ability to move forward in life. When you feel stressed, you are, in a way, stuck in fear: *False Evidence Appearing Real*. In that moment, you are disconnected from what really matters. Rubbing your knees gives you a moment to pause and receive a hands-on message to relax and *Be Here Now*.

I know it sounds simple—but give it a try. You will be surprised at how calming and nurturing it feels.

Louise Lavergne

Accessing the Power of Your Left and Right Brain – Your Nose Knows the Way

When you look at a drawing of the human brain, you notice that the brain is divided into two hemispheres. Each hemisphere processes information differently, has different jobs, and creates different experiences in our mind, body, and spirit. If you haven't seen brain researcher, Jill Bolte Taylor's, *Ted Talk*, I strongly recommend you watch it. In her book, *My Stroke of Insight: A Brain Scientist's Personal Journey*, she studied her own stroke as it happened. She shares her experience of each side of her brain. "Based upon my experience with losing my left mind," she explains, "I whole-heartedly believe that the feeling of deep inner peace is neurological circuitry located in our right brain."

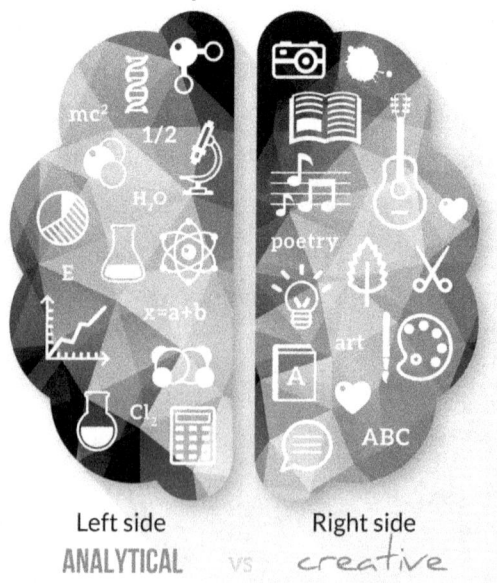

Two Hemispheres of the Brain

Left side
ANALYTICAL   vs   Right side
creative

Science shows us that the left brain performs tasks that have to do with logical, intellectual, analytical, and rational thinking. The left brain is responsible for controlling the right side of the body. The right hemisphere of the brain, on the other hand, performs tasks that have do with creativity, intuition, and all things that relate to feelings and hunches. The right brain coordinates the left side of the body. This is the science behind yogic breathing techniques, whereby you can regulate your brain by directing the flow of air, either drawing air in from the right or left nostril, or alternating, breathing through the right and left nostrils in turn. The left nostril connects to the right side of the brain (which induces relaxation), while the right nostril is associated with the left side of the brain (the more energizing side). You can see what part of your brain is dominant by noticing which nostril is blocked. If you wake up in the middle of the night and can't go back to sleep, there is a good chance your left nostril is blocked. You can help unblock your left nostril by lying on your right side and putting your left hand under your right arm pit. (Use your fist if you can—or put a small ball, like a tennis ball, in a sock.)

If, on the other hand, you need to be more alert and your right nostril is blocked, lean to the left and place your right hand in your left armpit.

Overall Benefits of Single or Alternate Nostril Breathing

Stilling the mind is crucial for effective problem-solving. Sometimes, you need to get calm and peaceful; other times, you need to be alert and energized. And sometimes, you need a bit of both!

Isolating each nostril when breathing has a profound effect on specific areas of your mind. Your left nostril communicates with your right brain, which lends itself to relaxation and re-connection. Your right nostril and left brain are buddies, and when they are engaged they can energize and revamp any situation.

Left Nostril

If you are breathing through your left nostril, it immediately calms your entire being. If you are feeling agitated or unfocused, left nostril breathing will help with your concentration by reducing your stress level. It will give you an overall feeling of relaxation and calm, diffusing any anxiety or tension you're feeling. Bonus! If you have trouble sleeping, this is a great tool to help you drift off.

Strategies – Use this Technique:

- When your mind is agitated and you want to relax or meditate.
- To help ease the chatter of your mind (like at the end of a busy day).
- To get peaceful, so you can tap into your intuition.
- Before doing a creative activity.
- To help you fall asleep (or if you wake up in the night and can't fall back into Dreamland).
- When you encounter a stressful situation (attending a work meeting, running late, seeing an ex), take time to pause and intentionally breathe through your left nostril.
- Three nights a week, plan to practice left-nostril breathing right before you go to sleep.

BE Break

BE Break: Practicing Left Nostril Breathing

- Make a fist with your right hand. Extend the index finger to block the right nostril.

- Inhale through your left nostril, breaking the breath into eight equal sniffs, filling your lungs completely on the eighth. Expand the abdomen. (Be careful not to take in too much air on the first sniffs.)

- Exhale in one long, smooth stroke, pulling in your abdomen.

- Your left hand should be relaxed in your lap, with the thumb and index finger touching (again, this mudra is called the "Gyan Mudra"). This hand position acts as a trigger to send a message to the body: Relax.

- Keep your spine straight. Feel the crown of your head reaching to the sky and feel your tailbone moving down, toward the ground. Your chin should be tucked in slightly (as if you were saluting someone).
- If sitting in a chair, make sure your legs are uncrossed, with both feet flat and resting firmly on the ground.
- You can use the sound "Sa-Ta-Na-Ma" twice, to count the eight sniffs on the intake.
- With your eyes barely open, try to focus at the tip of your nose. If it doesn't work for you, close your eyes and focus at the point between your eyebrows.

GYAN or CHIN MUDRA

Right Nostril

When you breathe through your right nostril (which is connected to your left, "analytical" brain), it revitalizes your body. It helps you to improve your alertness and awareness. Connecting with your right nostril breath boosts the nervous system (especially the parasympathetic nervous system) and at the same time, it supports digestion and increases overall vitality.

Strategies – Use this Technique:

- Before an important meeting or a stressful social situation.
- To improve clarity.
- When you are reading instructions or technical information.
- When writing or studying.
- When giving speeches, speaking in public, or teaching.
- When signing important documents.
- After eating, to help with digestion.
- Before you exercise.
- When you need to be alert and active.

BE Break

BE Break: Practicing Right Nostril Breathing

- Open your left hand. Use your thumb to block your left nostril.

- Inhale through your right nostril. Expand your abdomen and chest.

- Exhale completely and slowly, pulling your abdomen in.

- Your right hand should be relaxed in your lap. Bend your ring finger and press the thumb on top of it to hold it down. This mudra is called "Surya (Sun) Mudra" (see the image below). In yoga teachings, it is said that Surya Mudra enhances your vitality.

- Keep your spine straight. Feel the crown of your head reaching to the sky and your tailbone moving down toward the ground. Your chin should be tucked in slightly (as if you were saluting someone).
- Make sure your legs are uncrossed, with both feet flat and resting firmly on the ground.

SURYA or AGNI MUDRA

Alternate Nostril Breathing – Anuloma Viloma

Anuloma Viloma pranayam is designed to purify the psychic channels referred to in yogic terms as the *nadis*. In the yoga teachings, the two hemispheres of the brain (the right and left brain) are referred to as the Ida and Pingala nadis. "Nadi" comes from the Sanskrit root *nad*, meaning "channel" or "flow." The nadis are similar to meridians; they are the energetic channels through which your life force flows. This technique brings the two hemispheres of your brain into a harmonious relationship so you can access both your creative (right brain) and intellectual (left brain) gifts.

Benefits

Practicing breathing through one nostril at a time clears up blocked nostrils and cleanses and strengthens your whole respiratory system. It also calms the mind, making it lucid and peaceful as it helps you to clear away mental tension and worries. It also helps to relieve headaches and, if you practice it on regular basis, can even help reduce the occurrences of migraines.

As with all breath control practices, only do as much as you are comfortable with. Start slowly and build up steadily. Using a Neti pot prior to this practice is recommended. (A Neti pot is a small container with a long spout used to rinse the nasal cavities with a saline solution.)

BE Break

VISHNU MUDRA

BE Break: Practicing Alternate Nostril Breathing

- Keep your back straight, head up. Extend the torso so you are sitting tall.

- Feel your head being pulled up to the sky. Feel the base of your spine being pulled down to the center of the earth.

- Keep your chest open, your shoulders relaxed. Feel your shoulder blades and back dropping down gently.

- For your right hand, use the Vishnu Mudra (see below), by folding your index and middle fingers into your hand. Use your thumb to block the right nostril and the ring finger to block the left nostril.

- Your left hand should be relaxed in your lap. You can connect your thumb to the index and middle fingers (Gyan Mudra) to create supportive energy in your body for your practice.

- Start with the Three Life-Saving Breaths.

- Block your right nostril with your thumb. Start your first round by inhaling through the left nostril for four counts.

- Block both nostrils as you hold your breath for eight to sixteen counts.

- Release your thumb as you exhale through the right nostril for eight counts.

- Then, inhale through the right nostril for four counts. Again, block both nostrils.

- Hold the breath for eight to sixteen counts.

- Then, end the first round by releasing the ring finger and exhaling through the left nostril for eight counts.

  Start by practicing four rounds and build up to ten rounds.

End your practice with a few gentle breaths. If it feels challenging at first, be patient and compassionate with yourself. It will get easier the more you practice. Several clients have shared with me that by practicing this technique for three minutes a day, they saw significant improvement in their blood pressure.

The Brain – Gut Connection

> *"Truth is when your mind and your gut agree."*
> ~ Shannon Hale

Throughout your life, I'm sure you've experienced "butterflies in your stomach" or you've had "a gut feeling" about something. Or, perhaps you have gone through a "gut-wrenching" experience. Scientifically, we now know that your gut (or GI tract) is sensitive to feelings, and that any time you are experiencing intense emotion, you feel it in your gut. I talk about this in greater depth in my program, "Yoga to Love Your Gut."

In recent studies, a connection has been made that illuminates just how intertwined your brain and your gut really are. Your gut is made up of a lesser-known but equally-as-important nervous system as the one in your brain. Researchers now understand that this nervous system communicates directly with your brain. In fact, the information our gut relays to our bodies is so important that researchers have called the gut the "second brain" of the body.

That's why your mind has such a profound impact on your health, specifically as it relates to your digestion and gut-related issues. When you take the time to calm your mind and channel its power toward healing, miraculous things can start to take place in your body. Changing your thoughts and reducing your stress can help improve not just your digestion but also your overall health.

Accessing the Healing Power of Your Belly

Put your hand on your belly right now. What is the first thing that comes to your mind? When I ask that question in a group, I see most people frowning or knitting their brows. Do you think, "I should lose weight?" Or, do you feel guilty? ... "I shouldn't have eaten the whole Costco-size bag of chips last night." Your belly is a place that can trigger feelings that are all about "shoulds." But your belly is also where your power lies. Are you making an *Are you kidding me?* face right now? When you were an embryo in your mother's womb, you received everything you needed to become *you* through the umbilical cord. Your belly is where you hold your power. In yoga teachings, the belly is the location of your second chakra (which relates to creativity) and your third chakra (which relates to personal power). If you have any negative feelings toward your belly, take a moment now and apologize. You need a loving and peaceful relationship with this part of your body that does so much to contribute to your well-being. I'm going to show you how you can access some of this dormant energy in your belly any time you need an extra boost. This practice is a great way to increase energy, improve digestion, and tone the abdominal muscles. It is way more fun than doing sit-ups and you can do it in your fancy work clothes or your pajamas!

In yoga, Taoist, and martial arts teachings, the belly area is referred to as "the navel point." In my Kundalini yoga training I was taught that the navel point is located approximately two to three inches below your umbilicus. You can find this point by putting your four fingers on your belly below your belly button. In one of my Chi Gong trainings, I was told that the navel point is at the belly button itself. I have integrated the two points, the yogic and Taoist locations. You can form this triangle by touching the tips of both thumbs at your belly button, placing both hands at an angle, and touching the inside tips of your index fingers below. I like to imagine this shape as my Wonder Woman or Superman Super-Power belt buckle!

In my son's martial arts classes, the Hara or navel point was talked about as being the point in which you can access your center of gravity. If your belly is at peace, it will be easier for you to feel more balanced in your whole body and mind. I strongly encourage you to make this practice part of your daily BE Breaks.

In this exercise, you will be creating a pumping motion, as you pull the belly in and then release it out rhythmically. This exercise is called, "The Navel Pump."

BE Break

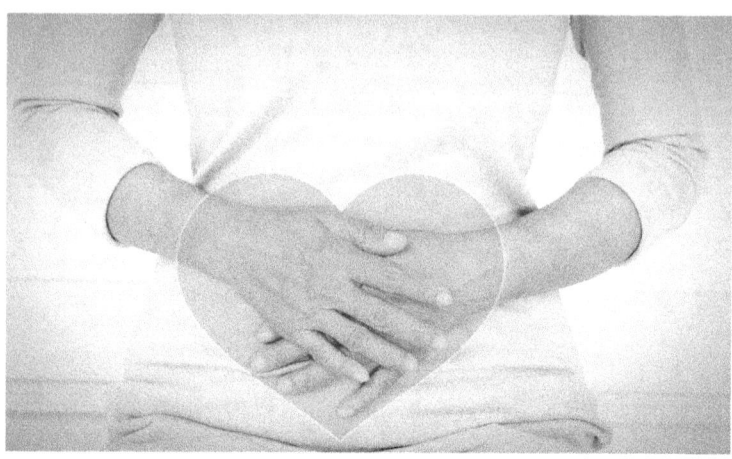

BE Break – Practicing the Navel Pump

Caution: *Do not practice the Navel Pump if you are pregnant or if you have had recent abdominal surgery. Always check with your Doctor or healthcare professional before engaging in any exercise program. Do not practice the Navel Pump on a full stomach. Women, do not do this exercise if you are in the first days of menses. Be gentle with Navel Pumps during your cycle.*

- When you first start this practice, it's a good idea to place your hands on your belly with thumbs meeting at the umbilicus.

- Inhale through your nose, feel the belly stretching out into your hands.

- As you hold your breath, pump your stomach by pulling your belly in and release it out. Start slowly, with just a few pumps per breath retention, then increase the rhythm and the number of pumps for each breath retention.

- When you cannot hold your breath any longer, exhale through your nose.

- Don't hold the breath longer than is comfortable for you. Just do the best you can.

- Continuing with another full breath in, fill your belly and chest, hold, and pump your navel in and out.

I used to do this sitting in the subway or on the bus in New York on my way to an audition, to help release the butterflies and increase my energy. I also use it before I go on stage to give a talk. It helps to turn nervous energy into useful, dynamic energy. Try to practice the Navel Pump for at least three breaths. Build from practicing a full minute and gradually increase up to three minutes. You can do this anywhere, anytime, but I recommend you practice this one in the morning and in the afternoon. This is a great caffeine-free, even gluten-and sugar-free solution to overcoming the afternoon slump and anytime you need a quick pick-me-up.

The Pelvic Breath – Your Gateway to Receiving and Letting Go

The pelvis and the lower part of your body, including your belly, legs, and feet, are all part of what relates in yoga and Ayurvedic medicine to the lower triangle, which includes energetic reference points referred to as the first, second, and third chakras. The lower triangle is where you initiate the feeling of security and balance in your whole body. Your desire to "stand on your own two feet" isn't really about standing—it's about feeling strong, secure, and powerful. Your *pelvic floor* is a group of muscles located in the "floor" of your pelvis; they support the entire pelvic area. The pelvic bones include the pubic bones in the front of your body, they extend out on each side to your hipbones and back to the tailbone (or coccyx) in your lower back. Within this diamond-like shape, your pelvic floor muscles form a sling to support your internal organs. These muscles have a great impact on elimination by helping the rectum and sex organ contract and release. Breathing also plays a huge part in supporting your ability to receive food, digest it, and let go of waste products through elimination. Like breathing, eating and pooping are crucial to survival.

I wrote earlier about the effect of 'doing and doing' leading you into Do-Do mode. The pelvic breath draws you into the physiology of the Do-Be-Do-Be-Do-Be rhythm. I designed a yoga practice called JoyFull Yoga, which is a "joy-full," integrated approach to self-healing that focuses on activating the glands and the lymphatic system and revitalizing the brain, lungs, and heart. It was birthed from the culmination of all my training, and heavily influenced by Chi Gong and Kundalini, and by Naam and Hatha yoga. In the beginning of a JoyFull yoga class we practice a variation of what I call "the pelvic breath," where your pelvic muscles team up with your diaphragm, core muscles, and lower back. It can help relieve and prevent back pain as well as prevent and improve issues of incontinence. I first learned about the power of the pelvic area from my training with Chi Gong Master, Mantak Chia. Since then I have read many medical reports supporting the information Master Chia shared with his students.

One of the most common pelvic floor strengthening exercises is called "Kegel" (you may have heard of it), named after its inventor, American gynecologist, Arnold Henry Kegel. A "Kegel" is a contraction of the pelvic floor muscles. To identify your pelvic floor muscles, stop urination in midstream or tighten the muscles that keep you from passing gas. What most people don't know about the Kegel exercise is the importance of combining it with the breath ... it's a loving partnership of breath, movement, and muscle contraction, to create a powerful, self-healing practice. For more information, please visit: www.joyfull-yoga.com and www.Foundation4yourLIFE.com

The pelvic breath is a crucial part of every JoyFull Yoga class. Here, I offer you the pelvic breath technique as another powerful BE Break—you can do it sitting, standing, or lying down. It's a great way to start your day—please see the supplemental videos at www.DoDoRescue.com.

Since your BE Breaks are going to happen mostly during your busy day, we'll focus on practicing sitting and standing.

BE Break

BE Break – Practicing the Pelvic Breath

Caution: In this exercise pregnant women should not hold the breath in or out. In the first three days of menses, women should only do gentle contractions.

- Start by standing (or sitting in a chair). Feel your feet planted firmly on the floor, press your toes and heels into the floor, and tighten your buttock muscles.

- Open your hands facing front, and relax them at your sides.

- Take a "full yogic breath" (see earlier), filling your belly and chest with air as you open your arms at your side in line with your hips and press back your arms to squeeze your shoulder blades.

- Bend your knees slightly as you arch your back, tailbone pressing back. Lift your chin slightly. This will open your whole chest cavity and make as much space as possible for your lungs to take in more air. As you pause with the in-breath, keep squeezing your shoulder blades toward your spine.

- As you feel the breath coming in, think about breathing in sunlight. Imagine sunlight filling your lungs, pausing with the in-breath to saturate every cell in your body with sunlight.

- On the exhale, straighten your legs, tuck your tail bone in, and release the pubic bones forward as you bring your hands back onto your belly. Pressing the belly in, contract the pelvic floor muscles and do a Kegel contraction, pulling the rectum, sex organ, and belly in toward the center of your body while holding the breath out* for three to ten counts. I like to think of the Kegel as an inner hug ... everything coming into the center of your being for a group hug.

- Repeat this for at least three breaths.

Your Heart: The Meeting Place for Your Mind and Your Gut to Make Peace

Your heart is where you experience the power of the physiology of your spirituality. Think of it as your personal healing room. Your physical and emotional heart holds the tremendous potential to help you balance your energy field, your physical body, and your life. The impact of what you feel is distributed to all the cells of your body through its physical function.

A few years ago, I heard an interview with best-selling author, Gregg Braden, a renowned pioneer in bridging science and spirituality. I was excited to hear him speak about several concepts that are similar to those on which my programs and classes are based: the power and the effects of creating coherence in our hearts. He talked about the fact that the brain's electrical and magnetic fields aren't anywhere near as powerful as the heart's. Braden says that:

> *The heart's electrical field is about 100 times stronger than that of the brain, and its magnetic field is about 5,000 times stronger than the brain's ... Our own physics textbooks say that if you want to change the atoms of physical matter, you have to change either the electrical field or the magnetic field; the heart does both.*

When you allow a positive thought of peace, gratitude, or love to settle in your heart and allow yourself to *"feel"* it, magic happens in your body. You can activate the feelings by slowing down the breath to slow down the mind—and then, as your heart rate improves, it can do the rest. Your stress levels go down, the function of your immune system improves, and you begin to feel an overall sense of well-being. Your heart is where your mind and your body can come together to create a magical coherence that can be so powerful, it can impact your life and even your surroundings.

In 1993, Quantum physicist, Dr. John Hagelin, led an experiment in which 4,000 people meditated together during what law enforcement considered to be a high crime period in Washington, D.C. The results of the experiment were published in the scientific journal *Social Indicators Research*. On that day, criminal activity decreased by 23.6%! They repeated this experiment forty-eight times in numerous venues, from inner-city schools, to prisons, to war-torn areas in countries such as Nicaragua and Iran, with remarkable results each time. When people hold a peaceful state, it creates a measurable field of "coherence." Similarly, in her books *The Field* and *The Intention Experiment*, author and researcher, Lynne McTaggart, speaks about the electrical and magnetic fields that connect all of life.

To feel better in an instant, all you have to do is to drop the attitude, and go into gratitude.

You can feel your way to better health and improve your work environment, your family, and the world around you by projecting positive emotions through your heart. Gregg Braden also talked about the importance of feelings. In an interview promoting his book *Resilience from the Heart*, Dr. Braden shared his experience of being with monks in a Tibetan monastery. He asked them what their tradition teaches about the force that connects everything in the Universe. He asked the abbot, "Is compassion a force of nature that connects everything in the Universe—or is it an experience that we have in our hearts?" The abbot answered with one word: "Yes."

If you are serious about living a balanced life in a peaceful world, you must start with yourself, by making a connection with your physical and emotional heart. This is what is referred to in the eastern teachings as the "heart center" or "heart chakra." If you want to start feeling better in an instant, all you have to do is drop the attitude and go into gratitude. By practicing gratitude, compassion, and love, you create the physical experience of inner peace ... and this brings us all a step closer to global peace.

CREATING POSITIVE COHERENCE

When your mind and your heart are in a tug-of-war, when you are upset about your job, when you do not know what to do about a problem, or when your mind and your gut can't agree, that's usually when fear slips right in. It gets into the driver's seat and takes you to freak-out town. But, you can avoid this trip. Here is a simple, yet effective BE Break to use as soon as you feel any discord. It will help you stop the tug-of-war and cultivate positive coherence within your heart space. It will create a respectful place for your feelings and your thoughts to meet while making healing space in your body and in your surroundings.

BE Break

BE Break – Uniting Your Thoughts and Feelings

Caution: In this exercise pregnant women should not hold the breath in or out.

Place your left hand at the center of your chest; your right hand below your navel, on your Super-Power belt buckle. If you can, close your eyes.

- Begin to slow down your breathing as you inhale slowly through your nose, into your chest and belly. Imagine your breath coming in through the center of your chest all the way down into your hips.

- Pause. If you can, hold that breath (*pregnant women, do not hold your breath) for four to ten counts and let the breath fill every cell in your body, all the way back up your spine, all the way up to your head.

- Exhale slowly as you gently pull your navel in.

- As you inhale, begin to think about one thing you are grateful for. Let yourself breathe that gratitude into your heart ... then let it fill your whole body as you hold your breath.

- On the exhale, imagine your breath coming out through the top of your head, sending a "Thank you" to the Universe (or to wherever or whomever you choose).

- If other thoughts of gratitude come up, bring them into your heart.

- As you end the exercise, take a moment to give thanks for the gift of showing up for yourself and for having the courage to be YOU in this moment.

- Let your heart embrace you with as much compassion as you can.

- You can also do this breathing exercise by breathing in peace or love and breathing it out.

- To enhance the practice, you can use the Sunlight, Divine Light, Peace prayer I shared in Chapter 3.

- Bring a smile to your face and gently open your eyes.

- Practice this exercise for at least one minute and for as long as you can.

The Healing Magic of the Cha-Cha-Cha

Part of my JoyFull Yoga class includes a moving meditation practice I call, "Dynamic Movement Meditation." It was inspired by a Chi Gong practice that stimulates the meridian points in the soles of the feet and by my love of movement. I sprinkled powerful yoga principles into it ... *and voila!* ... the combination of these healing practices creates a special kind of meditative experience that anyone can do successfully. The goal of the Dynamic Movement Meditation is not to do it perfectly, but to do your best, have fun, and practice not judging yourself. This meditation is a great opportunity to practice letting go of perfection and activating your sense of humor.

The healing purpose of the Dynamic Movement Meditation is to engage your lungs, heart, and glandular system and stimulate the lymphatic system in a fun way. Yes, I said *fun*! Fun is allowed—after all, it is called JoyFull Yoga. You can do it anytime you need a boost to energize yourself and release stress to feel great. I know that when I enjoy doing something, I am more likely to do it. It is a great way to support your body to release toxins and to create endorphins to boost your overall well-being by improving your circulation and brain function. It can be your daily "joyfull" ritual to de-stress and burn some calories at the same time.

I suggest you use the mantra Sa-Ta-Na-Ma to count the beats with your moves. I occasionally add a cha-cha-cha in between the Sa-Ta-Na Ma moves. When I do, I notice that my students smile and get even better results from the exercise. The sound of *tsh* or *ch* is part of the kidney healing sound *Chui* in one of the Chi Gong practices. The delight and smiles

I see on the participants' faces as they say and do the cha-cha-cha is powerful self-healing medicine. Repeating the sounds to the repetitive movements can create a meditative experience and helps you to stay focused and present as you balance the body and allow your mind to let go of negativity.

This is not necessarily the same exercise that I teach in class, but you can bring some of the crucial healing pieces into your own routine. I want to encourage you to make time to move every day in a way that is both fun and healing.

Use upbeat music with good words (or no words), but solid rhythm. I love using world music, but my all-time favorite is just about any song from Jesse Cook. He's a wonderful Canadian guitarist, composer, and producer. He incorporates elements of flamenco, jazz, and many forms of world music into his work. His music is so perfect for me, it's as if he's writing it for my JoyFull Yoga practice. Check out his *Rumba Foundation* or his *Beyond Borders*.

BE Break

LOUISE LAVERGNE

Sa Ta Na Ma

Cha Cha Cha

BE Break – The JoyFull Dynamic Movement Meditation

The most important part of this practice is to simply step (no need to trot) from right foot to left foot as you move your arms, hands, and hips.

March four steps forward to Sa-Ta-Na-Ma then double step to cha-cha-cha. Take four steps back, then stop to do another cha-cha-cha step. Four steps to the right — cha-cha-cha — then, four steps to the left — cha-cha-cha — and repeat as you go around your home. You can also pause and do the steps in one place, or even do the whole meditation sitting in a chair. The cha-cha-cha in between is optional. (If you can't use your feet, clap your hands on your body and/or on a cushion)

Shake your hands, your hips, or whatever you feel inspired to move. Just keep the Sa-Ta-Na-Ma rhythm going.

Do-Do Rescue

It is important to make it fun for yourself so you can get past any resistance and/or frustration or judgments that may show up about moving your body. I suggest you do at least three minutes, and up to ten minutes, daily. Five minutes seems to be a good goal to stay committed to. On super busy days, you can make it part of making dinner or even getting ready for work. Put on some happy music and dance on a regular basis. It can be a fabulous way to stay fit and connect to your joy.

To watch a variation of this JoyFull Movement Meditation, please visit www.DoDoRescue.com.

CHAPTER 5
GETTING STARTED WITH YOUR DO-BE-DO-BE-DO-BE LIFESTYLE

It has taken me years of practice (and it continues to be an ongoing practice) to stay connected to a balanced rhythm in my life. I have periods where I am inspired and "on it" and others that feel more like I'm carefully making my way across stepping stones in a raging river. But no matter what is happening in my life, there are three habits I stay committed to. I distinguish these habits from my general everyday routines by calling them "rituals." The word *ritual* implies an established set of procedures to mark a special occurrence. Creating a mindful ritual elevates any task or practice into something important and healing. Any action that supports your internal intention becomes a non-denominational prayer in motion.

A ritual requires three things:
1. Intention (For example): "I intend to create more peace in my body and in all areas of my life now."
2. Focus: Redirecting your mind to focus on your intention and to stay present for the duration of the ritual. (NOT looking at your phone or email.)

3. Effort: Setting a time and space for your ritual—and making it important enough to do it.

Three Morning Rituals to Change Your Life – One Day at a Time

Each commitment you are successful with helps to strengthen your mental and emotional muscles and sustain your supportive habits. Doing your rituals in the morning can set the tone for your whole day. The morning is also the detox period in your body's clock (called your *circadian rhythm*). It starts at four a.m. and continues until noon, making the morning the most effective time to commit to detox routines. Your body gives you the cue (usually within the first hour of waking up) when you feel the need to go to the bathroom. Of course, everybody's bathroom clock is different, but you can support your body's healthy detox process by engaging in the three rituals or habits outlined below.

My intention behind the detox approach is to release and clear all that is not serving my body and my mind now. I like the idea of making room in my body, and in my mind, and going into my day having created the space to attract and create all that supports me, my body, and my journey to be happy and healthy. These rituals are great ways to practice self-care in tangible, practical, and supportive ways. Through the years, I have had periods where my spiritual practice was disturbed because of travel or other obligations—but no matter what, I have kept these three rituals going. They help me get back on track with my Do-Be-Do-Be-Do-Be rhythm more easily. The first two relate to your body and the last one is a mind-centering practice to clear negativity and ignite your spirit to start your day more consciously, so you are prepared to make supportive choices.

These three morning rituals are simple and easy to commit to and can help you create a foundation for all your other supportive habits.

Morning Ritual #1 - Loving Your Tongue ~ and Feeling Terrific

An obvious place to start the detox process is in your mouth, specifically with your tongue, which plays an obscure but essential role in your overall well-being. The tongue is one of the most underrated and neglected organs in your body. Besides its crucial function in digestion, it is one of the most potent and effective organs to help detoxify your body and lower your stress levels.

Your tongue is one of your body's several detoxification paths. Keeping it clean is easy and is a crucial part of a health regimen. It merely requires using a tongue scraper: an inexpensive, V-shaped, thin (ideally, stainless steel) tool. Using a tongue scraper is part of my daily routine that I learned in my Ayurvedic training. This simple practice has been scientifically proven to help remove bacteria and toxins (otherwise called "gunk") that we experience as bad breath or cotton mouth. Brushing your tongue with a toothbrush will only relocate the bacteria or embed them in your toothbrush rather than removing them. It's best to use a tongue scraper first (or the edge of a spoon works well), then, brush your teeth as usual.

Detoxification is just one of the benefits of tongue scraping. Removing gunk and phlegm will also improve your overall sense of taste and digestion, because as you scrape you are gently massaging the internal organs linked to different areas of the tongue, as well as activating the salivary glands. I remember an Ayurvedic doctor telling us during one of my yoga teacher trainings that as you reach the back of your tongue, it can cause your eyes to water. For me, it triggers the gag reflex (which I dislike strongly enough to not want to do it), but I remember him saying that the "tears" that accompany the gag reflex contain enzymes that are beneficial for cleaning your eyes and preventing cataracts. That has stayed with me as my motivating factor. In my early twenties, the removal of gunk and bad breath was a strong motivation for tongue scraping, but over the years, I've come to appreciate all the extra benefits this simple hygiene habit has given me.

For Morning Ritual #1, there are two other yogic practices involving your tongue that are simple yet powerful techniques to help detox and de-stress your body. Each one can be practiced as a BE Break anytime you have some time to yourself during the day.

The first one you can learn from your dog.

Dog Breath:
Dogs know the benefits of panting. Ever notice how happy your dog looks when it is panting? For humans, it is also a great way not only to move toxins, but to stimulate your immune system. Stick your tongue out and practice breathing in and out in equal segments. Put a hand on your belly—feel the belly stretching out as you breathe in and pulling toward your spine as you breathe out. Start slowly and increase the rhythm as you are able to. Stay connected to the movement in your belly. Keep your breathing even and light. Don't try to take deep breaths. Watch a dog do it and learn. They are masters of this technique.

Cat Purr:

Cats know this secret, but unlike dogs, they are more mysterious about how they do it. They give you a blissful gaze as they purr into deep relaxation. They know that purring is an excellent way to relieve stress. Your tongue, like any other muscle, holds tension. Try purring by making a breathy rhrhrhrrrrrr sound. It may require practice. The more you relax your tongue, the easier it gets. You can also tap the tip of your tongue to the roof of your mouth with a "da da da da" or "la la la la" on the out-breath. Try to alternate those two sounds as fast as you can. (Go ahead and laugh if it feels funny. Laughing is fantastic for your overall nervous system) Stimulating the acupuncture points located at the tip of your tongue and the two ridges behind your front teeth activates the meridians (or channels of energy) that relate to the hypothalamus and the pineal gland, which regulate the endocrine system. Try it the next time you feel stressed. You will begin to understand the wisdom of our feline friends.

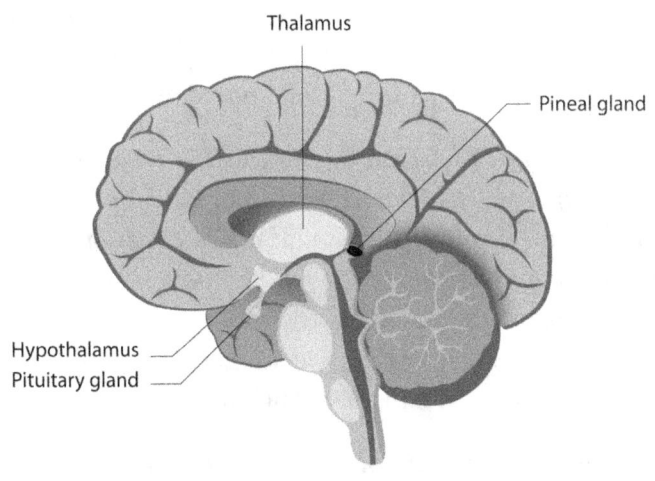

Morning Ritual #2 - Loving Your Gut ~ and Feeling Great

This ritual can make you feel grand. After cleaning your tongue, drink a glass of water (10 ounces) with lemon juice and a dash of sea salt (omit the salt if you have blood pressure issues or if you are on a sodium-restricted diet). Lemon juice alone is a good source of vitamin C (which is good for your immune system) and potassium (which is supportive for blood pressure). An interesting fact about lemon is that although it is acidic on its own, when you put it in water and drink it, it turns alkaline, which is very beneficial for the body. If you don't like lemons, you can use limes if you prefer. Limes are slightly lower in vitamin C, but limes will do the same thing as lemons to help eliminate toxins.

For this ritual, I use room temperature, purified water. If you don't have good filtered water, you can boil water the night before and it will be at room temperature in the morning. You can also use warm or hot water. I prefer to avoid cold water—as these rituals are to support the body's detoxification process, drinking warm or room temperature water seems kinder to my body. The best temperature for you is the one you are going to use daily. If you hate warm water, better to drink it cold than not to drink it at all.

I use one half of a lemon when I can, but it's a good idea to start with a quarter lemon and see how it is for you. I squeeze the lemon juice into a glass and add a pinch of sea salt. I like the pink Himalayan sea salt best because it has terrific healthy minerals. Stir to dissolve most of the salt, then add warm or room temperature water and stir until all the salt is dissolved. Take a breath, then slowly drink the water.

For me, the other big plus of this ritual is liver support. The liver processes all the toxins in your body, and it's your *emotional filter. It's where unresolved anger sits—and anger is a close relative of frustration and resistance. Drinking my glass of lemon (or lime) water within the first thirty minutes of my day clears any lingering obstacles in my physical and emotional body. I do it every day and I feel good about staying committed to my self-care.*

So, now that we have taken loving care of our mouths and guts—this next ritual is for your mind.

Morning Ritual #3 - Loving your Mind ~ Three-Minute Mind Shower

After you take your morning shower, taking a few minutes for a mind bath is a great way to start your Do-Be-Do-Be-Do-Be day. It's sometimes challenging to restrain your mind from jumping into the Do-Do of the day, so giving your day a head start with this great BE practice can help prevent a Do-Do day. I learned this effective and quick way to clean the mind from my Kundalini Master Teacher, Yogi Bhajan, many years ago. When he taught it, he mentioned that the Buddha had taught this technique to his disciples to help still the overactive mind. I'm not sure about the historical reference, but I know that it works for me. I love that it only takes three minutes to feel its full effect. Of course, you can use this as a BE Break anytime during your day, but I recommend you commit to doing it at the start of each day to quickly and effectively set your intentions for your day. This is my go-to meditation when I am short on time. If you are new to the idea of a morning practice, this could a great way to get started for the first forty days of your Do-Be-Do-Be-Do-Be lifestyle.

To get the most out of this practice, I suggest that before you get into the practice, you write on a blank page: "My intention(s) for today is / are _____.

Claim the opportunity to stay committed and avoid extended periods of coasting in the "good enough" trap. I need to remind myself that I am always just a "Do" away from a Do-Do day. This ritual doesn't have to be a long process and you don't need to write a long list.

Here are a few suggestions you can use for your intention:
1. *"My intention for today is to be in alignment with ALL that supports my Higher good and my part within the Higher good of All."*
2. *"My intention for today is to do my best, speak my truth, and practice meeting myself, my challenges, and others with kindness."*
3. *"I am complete and one with Divine Source Energy and I align my actions for today to be supportive of my Higher good and the Higher good of All."*

Then, proceed with the Mind Shower Practice to clean and clear your mind.

The Practice:

Mudra: The hand gesture you will use for this exercise is called the Man Suhaavee Mudra. It roughly translates to "the mudra that pleases the mind." "Man" in Sanskrit means mind. It helps to calm your mind in just three minutes. It is also called the Kalesvara Mudra. By either name, it is known for its powerful mind-calming benefits. To get into it, bend your elbows and bring your hands up to meet in front of your body, in line with the chest. Hold your hands about two to four inches away from your body. Hold your elbows just a little lower than your hands. Bend your index (Jupiter) fingers of each hand in toward the palms, and press them together along the second knuckle. Extend your middle (Saturn) fingers and let the fingertips meet, pointing away from you. Curl the

DO-DO RESCUE

ring (Sun) and little (Mercury) fingers into your hand. Join your thumb tips (Mars) pointing toward you. Thumbs point toward you; the middle fingers point away from you.

MAN SUHAAVEE
or
KALESVARA MUDRA

Your Breathing:

You can do slow, deep "yogic" breaths as you learned in the Three Life-Saving Breaths section earlier. Take a short pause after both the breath in and the breath out.

YOUR FOCUS AND VISUALIZATION:

OPTION 1: *Using an Affirmation:*
You can repeat a phrase mentally to engage your mind with the cleansing process.
For the Inhale:
Imagine filling your mind with sunlight.
Say the phrase: "I align with my truth."

Pausing with the inhale, say:
"I clear all the thoughts that are not supporting my Higher good now."

As you pause with the breath in, imagine your brain being bathed in sunlight.

For the exhale, say the phrase:
  "I release and clear my mind now. Thank you."

You could also simply repeat the word "Release" three times.

Pause with the exhale, and say:
  "I release and clear all negativity from my mind and body."

OPTION 2: *Using a Sound Current (Mantra) to Regulate the Breath:* Earlier, I introduced you to the sound current of Sa-Ta-Na-Ma.

Sa-Ta-Na-Ma is like the four seasons, or the full circle of life. You can use it to keep your mind focused on clearing and releasing any negativity. You can lengthen your vowels like this: "Saa-Taa-Naa-Maa" to keep the breath slow and smooth.

You can visualize each sound as a little sparkle of light to reconnect you with what is truly important to you. Use the word "Release" on the breath out, as mentioned above.

Practicing the Mind Shower using Sa-Ta-Na-Ma:

With your hands in the Man Suhaavee mudra, close your eyes and count slowly as you breathe in, mentally saying, "Saa-Taa-Naa-Maa." Then, pause and repeat mentally, "Sa-Ta-Na-Ma." Or, you can mentally say, "I align with my Truth." Then, exhale

DO-DO RESCUE

slowly with the same mantra, "Saa-Taa-Naa-Maa." Or, use the phrase, "I am that I am." To get the most out of this practice, repeat this breathing pattern for at least one minute and build up to three minutes.

You can combine these two options and come up with what will work best for you. Keep it simple at first. Three minutes is the maximum time recommended for this impactful mind shower practice with the Man Suhaavee Mudra.

These three-morning rituals can be integrated easily into your morning routine. They will give you a great foundation to sustaining a healthy, happy Do-Be-Do-Be-Do-Be lifestyle.

CHAPTER 6
SWEET DREAMS ~
<u>SWEET LIFE</u>

A Good Night's Sleep Can Improve Your Day

The Centers for Disease Control and Prevention (CDC) reported last year that more than a third of Americans don't get enough sleep. Many health issues like depression, autoimmune disorders, and memory issues have a connection to insufficient sleep. Harvard medical researchers have also linked sleep deprivation to obesity, high blood pressure, and daytime fatigue. Most of us have experienced not sleeping well on occasion. Stress, worry, staying up too late, eating late, or sleeping on a bad mattress can all be contributing factors. Over time, not getting enough sleep can be detrimental to your health.

The American Academy of Sleep Medicine and the Sleep Research Society recommend that adults aged eighteen to sixty years sleep seven to eight hours each night to maintain optimal health and well-being. Studies have shown that those over sixty may need one hour less. Professor of Sleep and Physiology and Director of the Surrey Sleep Research

Centre, Derk-Jan Dijk, Ph.D., stated the obvious: "Whether you are young or old, if you are sleepy during the day you either don't get enough sleep or you may suffer from a sleep disorder."

For some people, an occasional sleeping pill can do the trick, but if you take them daily they become less effective, so you need to take more and more. Taking sleeping aids can also become addictive, and the habit can prevent you from dealing with core issues and keep you stuck in unhealthy patterns. If you need more motivation to stop the sleeping pill habit, new research also shows that long-term use of certain kinds of sleeping pills may contribute to dementia and Alzheimer's. Learning to cultivate inner peace is a crucial part of the Do-Be-Do-Be-Do-Be lifestyle and is an excellent drug-free antidote for sleep deprivation.

Like other challenges in life, when you take responsibility and take preventative and supportive measures to help resolve sleep issues, you can create long-term solutions to improve your well- being and quality of life. Dr. Wayne Giles, Director of CDC's Division of Population Health, recommends that you make getting enough sleep a priority and he stresses the importance of making lifestyle changes that support good sleep habits. The Do-Be-Do-Be-Do-Be lifestyle sets you up to be ready for deep sleep by the end of your day. An additional nighttime routine can make a massive difference in the quality of your sleep.

I have created an online program called Peace of Heart & Soul for Deep Healing Sleep. It includes guided relaxation, yoga and meditation practices, and lifestyle tips to support you to get a good, healing night's sleep. Participants have reported not only sleeping better, but seeing significant improvements in their overall well-being goals. They were less grumpy and more patient with their kids and co-workers.

Also, people on weight loss diets found that they experienced better results when they were getting enough sleep. A good night's sleep is a precious gift you can give yourself. It is one of the best preventative measures to maintain vibrant health. After practicing your BE Breaks regularly, you may notice that your sleep improves.

Sweet Dreams: The Best Night Time Ritual to Start With

When you come to the end of your day, the last thing you want is another thing to do, I know, BUT this one is worth the effort. Rub your feet before going to bed with a relaxing lotion or oil that contains essential oils like Jatamansi (Spikenard), Lavender, Frankincense, Marjoram, or Ylang Ylang. Avoid citrus scents like Grapefruit and Orange as they are stimulating. As with the hands, the feet have several meridian points that relate to all the organs and systems of your body. Without getting into anything specific, the simple act of massaging your feet can be an enjoyable self-care ritual that fosters compassion and self-love. Because of the acupuncture points in your feet, you are tending to your whole body. As you massage your feet, you can give thanks to your body for its support and comfort during the day. It's worth making this practice part of your daily rituals for forty days. You can end by massaging your hands as well.

Because sleep is a crucial part of your success in creating a balanced Do-Be-Do-Be-Do-Be lifestyle, I want to share with you a few more tips to support you in getting a good night's sleep:

- *Avoid over-eating at night and don't eat after 8:00 p.m.*

- *Turn off all electronic devices, including the TV (and avoid watching the late-night news) one hour before going to sleep.*
- *Write down anything you want to remember for the next day, so you don't have to lie awake thinking about it. Take a look at my Three Lists System below.*
- *Practice a few minutes of slow, deep breathing through your left nostril. As I mentioned earlier, this enhances the right brain function, which induces relaxation and eases the chatter of the left brain.*
- *One of my favorite bedtime rituals is to drink a cup of golden milk one hour before bed.*

Golden milk is an anti-inflammatory yogic recipe that helps lower blood pressure and sugar levels and helps detox your liver. It also boosts your immune system and eases your digestive system—all of which helps you to get to sleep faster. You can find several variations of golden milk recipes on the internet. I am so passionate about the healing benefits of golden milk that I have included the recipe I use below. It is a bit time-consuming and messy to make, so I like to make enough to last at least a couple of weeks. Be forewarned: making the paste can be a messy job, and turmeric stains.

To make the golden paste:
- 1/4 cup organic turmeric powder
- 1 cup water
- 1/2 teaspoon black pepper or a few peppercorns
- 1/4 cup (more or less to taste) of grated fresh ginger root
- 2 1/2 tablespoons organic virgin coconut oil.

I also like to add one teaspoon of Ceylon cinnamon. (Be aware that regular cinnamon can be toxic in large quantities. Read your labels. If you can't find Ceylon cinnamon, I suggest you skip it.) If you want, you can add a few drops of vanilla.

Use a stainless-steel pot, mix everything, and bring it to a simmer as you stir for seven minutes, or until it turns into a paste.

Put the paste into a clean glass jar, let cool, and refrigerate. It should last two to three weeks.

When you are ready to drink your golden milk, heat a cup of milk of your choice (I like coconut milk). Then, add a teaspoon of golden paste. Stir and strain into your favorite mug. You can sweeten to your taste with a little honey, agave, or gut-healing Yacon syrup. As you prepare your golden milk, set your intention for a restful sleep. For me, this ritual is well-worth the effort and I include it in my life whenever I can.

THE THREE LISTS SYSTEM

When you do the above breathing exercises and mindful practices regularly, you'll find yourself automatically stepping out of Do-Do Mode and into the Do-Be-Do-Be-Do-Be system of relaxation and balance. You'll face life's challenges, complications, and chaos more easily. Your BE Breaks will help you to be grounded, to shift your focus, and to direct your energies so you can rise above the stressors of everyday life. Your BE Breaks will guide you gently onto a more productive—and hence more prosperous—path, connected with your true purpose and engaged with the heart-centered part of you that knows how to interact meaningfully with others, attain your dreams, and tap into your greatest potential. You'll reclaim your vitality, restore your health, and feel inspired, uplifted, and energized as you move forward with each busy day. When you dedicate yourself to taking regular BE Breaks—no matter where you are or what you are doing—you'll live your life with more clarity and calmness, consciously managing each stressor with grace and compassion.

Your Self-Care Priorities List:

Include all the things you can do to take better care of yourself. You can organize this list into three categories. Yoga and Chi Gong are some of the practices that can fit into all three categories.

- *Mind:* Engaging in meditation, yoga, positive thinking, or deep breathing for three to five minutes (good for mind and body), doing a crossword puzzle, etc.
- *Body:* Doing any exercise you enjoy, including walking, going to yoga class, eating healthy foods, etc.
- *Spirit:* Reading inspirational material, praying, taking time to meditate or practice yoga, doing service or volunteer work.

Your Joy and Fun List:

Write down all the things that bring you joy. Take time to add to your list at least once a month. You can organize this list into two categories as noted below. Schedule at least one thing from this list a month—but ideally, include one each day!

- *Spontaneous Activities*: Take a bubble bath, spend time with family/friends, take time to read or to watch a funny movie, etc.

- *Planned or special events:* Take a walk on the beach, attend a social gathering with friends, plan trips you might like to take, etc.

Your Daily To-Do List:

A good time to create your daily to-do list is before going to bed at night, when all is quiet. Using a page from an agenda with time blocks will help you see when you have time available to fit everything in. As you make space in your daily ritual to create this to-do list, it will help you to clear your mind and to set a realistic schedule for each day. Remember, this is a *practice*. It will take time for you to get better at not over-scheduling events and meetings. As you create your daily to-do list, be sure to include a minimum of one thing from each of your "Self-Care Priorities List" categories: Mind, Body, and Spirit. Each evening, write down scheduled pick-ups, drop-offs, deadlines, events, and meetings for the following day, adding in any unfinished business from today if still appropriate. Include at least one Spontaneous Activity from your "Joy and Fun" List.

As you are planning your daily to-do list, avoid cramming in too many things. A good rule of thumb is that if it can't fit on one page, it may be that you have over-scheduled your day. Be compassionate with yourself. Compassion is one of the keys to tranquility and peace of mind—would you feel okay about asking another person to do that much in a day? Also, allow yourself plenty of time to get from one activity, event, or meeting to another. That alone will reduce your stress levels considerably.

I encourage you to start a journal to keep track of your progress with this life-affirming, life-changing Do-Be-Do-Be-Do-Be system. Be sure to include the "Three Lists System"

above at the start of your journal. Some of the activities on your list may seem obvious to you now, but when you find yourself in a funk or if you're stressed, it's easy to forget what to do. Keeping your list handy will assist you in creating more joy, happiness, and peace in your day and in your life.

You can quickly refer to your list whenever you need to lower your stress level. (Also, when you discover a new activity or you get a new idea, don't forget to add it to your list.)

It's amazing what can happen when you create space in your day for BE Breaks. Because you've made your lists, you won't be preoccupied with thinking about all the things you have to get done and you will have more time to enjoy your day. You may even sleep better at night. As you become more in charge of how you navigate your day, it is important to also pay attention to what you are thinking, and then decide if those thoughts are creating the kind of life you want to create. If they are not, *change your thoughts*. Remember too, feel gratitude often. Gratitude expresses courage and it spreads calm, so take the time to think about what you are grateful for throughout your day, every day.

As you begin your Do-Be-Do-Be-Do-Be transformation, you can click on the link below to access bonus material designed to help you practice your BE Breaks and unlock even more harmony, calm, and clarity in your life: www.DoDoRescue.com.

Every time you take a BE Break, you can cultivate a peaceful mind and lower your stress level—both of which are giant steps toward a healthier, more fulfilling lifestyle. When you are ready to explore more ways to support your inner journey, I invite you to accelerate your progress by tapping into other programs at **www.Foundation4yourLIFE.com**.

CHAPTER 7
GET IN THE DRIVER'S SEAT ~ BECOME THE HEALER OF YOUR LIFE

Within just a few weeks of embracing the Do-Be-Do-Be-Do-Be model, you'll be making quantum leaps toward living a more balanced life. The Do-Be-Do-Be-Do-Be system continues to be a practice for me and I keep reminding myself that a practice is not about perfection. My New York Do-Do life propelled me into a deeper level of commitment to create balance in my body. I left New York over fifteen years ago, when I "Do-Be-Do-Be-Do-Beed" my way to the west coast. The journey has not been without a few Do-Do periods here and there, but practicing the Do-Be-Do-Be-Do-Be lifestyle makes it easier to get out of Do-Do. My west coast years have been about coming into my power and committing to inner peace in a whole new way. It continues to be about maintaining balance in my body *and* in my day-to-day life.

This book is my "Eastside" story—and in my next book, I'll share my "Westside" story. There are three births in that story (my beautiful daughter, JoyFull Yoga, and www.Foundation4yourLIFE.com) and many dramas and triumphs. Living a peaceful life includes some bumps in the road and still to this day (and most recently, through the process of writing this book), the BE Breaks are what keep me smiling and thriving. My life is still crazy-busy, but I'm now living by design, not by default—and I love every part of it. I know that this system and the related BE Breaks will help you move far beyond the limitations of stress-related frustration, overwhelm, and anxiety. Day by day, it can guide you into a brand-new phase of life that will bring you the freedom to be your authentic, confident self and live life to your fullest potential.

I look forward to seeing you on my www.DoDoRescue.com website. I am creating support material to help you stay engaged with your BE Breaks ... and more. When you are ready to engage in an even deeper conversation about moving beyond limitations and balancing your physical body and your spiritual nature, and when you feel the call to go deeper into your soul's purpose journey, please read my "Westside" story in my new book, *The Missing Peace*.

I am wishing you every success in living more fully from your heart, tapping into your deepest joy, and awakening fully to your amazing inner wisdom through using the Do-Be-Do-Be-Do-Be system. Many blessings to you as you embrace your passion, power, and purpose!

CHOICE is the most powerful tool you have...

Your reality is the sum of the choices you make, moment-by-moment.

Your life is a field of infinite possibilities.

Every choice you make can open or shut an infinite number of doors.

In every moment and with every breath you take, you can change the direction of your day and of your LIFE by making a simple choice.

It is all in your hands, in your heart, and in your mind...

What are YOU choosing right now?

It is my wish for you that your BE Breaks help you to make the most of your gift of choice.

I wish you peace of heart and clarity of mind to make choices that support YOU and your Higher good TODAY!

Scientists are ... leading us to a final realization, through validation, of what spiritual masters have known for centuries. That we are a lot more than we seem, that we are all part of a whole, that we have far greater extended potential than we make use of or understand.

~ Lynne McTaggart

AFTERWORD

by Tammey Violeta

I met Louise in December, 2001 when she presented her corporate stress management program, Yoga on the Go, at New York Life Insurance's New York headquarters. I had just started working there as a Call Center Rep. It was post-9/11. As a nation, we were feeling lost. My personal life was in transition. I had finally landed a job after being laid off earlier in the year, my mother had recently passed, and I was a newly-single mom with a six-year-old daughter. I felt ill-equipped to provide my little girl with a sense of security when everything around us had fallen apart, including the world outside of our home.

Listening to Louise's talk, I felt inspired and encouraged. Could it really be that simple? She made it so easy to follow her guidance and do the exercises. There was something about Louise's energy. Her techniques were clear and her strategies empowered me to feel like "I can do this!" Her program gave me hope. She showed up in my life that day with her bright light and a wonderful thing happened. Much like one uses one candle to light another, her light ignited mine.

When I first decided to take Louise's Yoga on the Go program, I didn't know how I'd pay for it or how I'd have the time for a weekly class, but I felt called to take that first step.

The practices were all foreign to me and as I'm an introvert, this was out of my comfort zone. But given that everything I knew had changed, trying something new seemed like a good option.

Back then, everything I did was for my daughter. Her well-being is what motivated me. I wanted to be a better me so I could be a better mom. At the time, I was overwhelmed. I was dealing with the stress of my new job during the day and going to night school to get my Bachelor's degree to improve my job options. I was trying to be a good mom while trying not to have a breakdown over being alone, divorced, and mourning the death of my mom.

At first, the biggest challenge for me was finding the time to attend Louise's sessions at New York Life. (In those days, she didn't have on-line programs.) Making time during my work day, once a week, was all I could manage. I looked forward to her classes; I always felt so good and inspired after each session. It was the only "me" time I had. As a Call Representative, my work schedule was not my own, and as work got busier, attending group sessions was becoming less of an option. This turned out to be a gift because I made an appointment to work with Louise one-on-one. Those sessions changed my life.

Louise helped me through all my layers and layers of "Do-Do." I resisted the Do-Be-Do-Be-Do-Be lifestyle a LOT. It wasn't easy to break my habits of doing and avoiding and numbing. I was able to work my way up the corporate ladder and with every promotion, there were challenges. But Louise inspired me and guided me to keep living up to being the best version of myself, even though my life continued to be busy. She helped me get to the root of the blocks that were keeping me stuck. Her guidance and wisdom nurtured me through my self-healing journey—to live a successful and balanced life.

Louise's unconditional support and compassion helped me to stop being so hard on myself and opened me to meet myself as I am, with a lot of compassion, love, and forgiveness.

She also helped me to create time for me to meet myself within my super-busy schedule. I've come to appreciate that my daily practice is part of me learning to truly love myself. Louise continues to remind me that "Self-Care is Self-Love." The amazing thing is that the more I take the time to rebalance throughout my day, the better I feel, and I can produce my best work for my company.

So, here we are, years later, and I still have a daily practice. It's evolved over time, sometimes it's just sitting down to do the "Three Life-Saving Breaths" you learned in this book. I use BE Breaks throughout my workday as well. I use a BE Break before meetings, before difficult conversations, and after difficult situations. I use a BE Break whenever I step outside of my comfort zone. And boy, have I stepped out of my comfort zone—it has been so rewarding! I now live in Dallas, TX; I'm a Corporate Vice-President (still with New York Life); I get to travel for work; and I went from the corner office to having the freedom to work from home. I love my Do-Be-Do-Be-Do-Be lifestyle!

My work with Louise has given me the confidence to be an inspiring mentor to my team and help them apply some of Louise's life-changing practices. As an introvert, this is HUGE! I get to watch them move on to great things themselves. Louise has empowered me to be the healer of my life and take responsibility to co-create with the Universe a life that I love and thrive in.

I feel grateful to be part of Louise's Master group coaching program, and whether it's through one of her on-line coaching programs, one-on-one, or attending one of her retreats, Louise continues to inspire me. Whenever I'm in "crisis" mode (aka *fear*), she offers me unconditional support and compassion. She helps me see through the fog of confusion by giving me clear inspiration and an actionable resolve (such as a practice), or suggesting a helpful remedy based on her vast training. Her well of wisdom runs deep and her intuition is spot on. It's amazing—as soon as I reach out to book a session, I can feel her supportive energy. My day begins and often ends with one of the meditations from Louise's online programs. I structure my days of the week based on what she has taught me about the planetary influences from her Universal Kabbalah classes.

I am proud of all that I have overcome and accomplished, but what I am most grateful for is how I have grown on the inside. As much as I love my daughter, she is no longer my primary motivation to be my best self. I am motivated by ME ... my relationship to myself, my body, and my spirit. It all started by learning the basics of a Do-Be-Do-Be-Do-Be lifestyle. I now move through the world from a place of strength, empowerment, and joy. Louise continues to remind me that in order for me to remain this way, I need to keep showing up for myself. I must be consistent with my practice, which is now all about self-love.

I have been a part of many of Louise's programs. With each one, I get to heal more and feel more joy in my life. I keep learning and adding new tools to my toolbelt (it's more like an entire tool chest). I get to revisit them often and use them as needed.

In short, Louise's work is integrated throughout my day-to-day life. It's been a blessing for me, and continues to be one. I hope that it will be for you too. In this book, Louise gives you the tools to begin your own Do-Be-Do-Be-Do-Be lifestyle. She has taken the wisdom from her various teachings and delivered them in bite-sized pieces. She makes it easy for us to stay committed. BE Breaks are simple but deep—and they work! Thanks to the practices Louise shares

Do-Do Rescue

in this book, I am able to flow through my days with peace and ease, regardless of what shows up. I desire the same for you.

As you have learned in this book, when you do things for your higher good, you are also doing it for the Higher good of all. We live in a time of uncertainty, and Louise has taught me that if you feel overwhelmed and unsure of what to do to help the world, start with yourself.

> *"The biggest changes in your life come from each moment that you choose to break out of the drama, the worry, or the fear by practicing a BE Break. Each of these moments mark a transition. Each transition is a step forward and creates the staircase that leads you to your transformation. With each choice and each breath, you can set yourself FREE."*

You can be the calm in the storm by practicing a BE Break in the moment. As Louise says, "The biggest changes in your life come from each moment that you choose to break out of the drama, the worry, or the fear by practicing a BE Break. Each of these moments mark a transition. Each transition is a step forward and creates the staircase that leads you to your transformation. With each choice and each breath, you can set yourself FREE." When you practice creating inner peace, you change your vibration. When you change your vibration, you change the vibration of everyone you encounter that day ... and so on. That's how I serve. That's how you can serve too. I am honored to call Louise my mentor, my spiritual coach, and my friend. I am truly excited to see her beautiful work put out in the world so that it can reach an even larger audience. Finally, I am excited for you to use these wonderful practices so you too can experience the joy and success of living a balanced life.

With Love and Light,
~ Tammey Violeta

ABOUT THE AUTHOR

Louise Lavergne is an author, a spiritual teacher, and an international speaker in the field of personal growth and empowerment. She offers effective and transformative tools, guidance, and inspiration so you can reclaim your power and become the healer of your life. Blending scientific and mystical elements, she creates a bridge from ancient wisdom to modern technology to help her clients address the challenges of our twenty-first century lifestyles.

Louise's wisdom is the culmination of thirty-five years of experience in personal development and metaphysical studies, including Universal Kabbalah, Chi Gong, Ayurveda, meditation, and yoga. She is the creator of JoyFull Yoga, an invigorating, restorative, and deeply healing yoga practice. Each class is unique, designed to engage your body, mind, and spirit on a self-healing journey through breath work, sound, movement, and asanas (yoga poses), leaving you with a lasting sense of presence and well-being, inside and out. Louise shares some of the elements of JoyFull Yoga in this new book, Do-Do Rescue. For more information on classes and events, please visit joyfull-yoga.com.

Louise is the CEO of Foundation4YourLIFE.com, an online wellness coaching center that offers a range of online classes and coaching programs designed to support you to live a truly inspired life, deepen your relationship with yourself, and live in harmony with your life's purpose. Each program offers you tools to manage and reduce stress and to overcome fears, blocks, and self-limitations so you can improve your spiritual and emotional well-being.

Louise amusingly refers to herself as a spiritual sanitation engineer. "There is nothing about you that needs to be fixed," she says. "We're here to clean up and heal. Once you are in a healing relationship with yourself, the fog clears. You can then fully embrace your soul purpose to align with your authentic self. It's all about the life-long quest to BE unconditional love."

Louise lives in Southern Oregon. She enjoys spending time with her family, including her two cats, Max and k.d. (named after one of her favorite artists, k.d. lang), and the best dog ever, Bramble. She loves traveling and creating new programs to support you. She is working on her next book, The Missing Peace.

BIBLIOGRAPHY

Bach, Richard. *Illusions: The Adventures of a Reluctant Messiah*. New York: Dell Publishing, 1977. Print.

Chia, Mantak. *Awaken Healing Energy Through the Tao: The Taoist Secret of Circulating Internal Power*. First Edition. Santa Fe: Aurora Press, 1991. Print.

Healing Light of the Tao: Foundational Practices to Awaken Chi Energy. First Edition. New York: Simon and Schuster, 2008. Print.

The Inner Smile. New York: Simon and Schuster, 2008. Print.

Coué, Émile. *Self Mastery Through Conscious Autosuggestion*. New York: American Library Service, 1922. Print.

Hạnh, Thích Nhất. *Being Peace*. Arnold Kotler, Ed. Berkeley: Parallax Press, 1987. Print. Kegel, Arnold Henry. https://en.wikipedia.org/wiki/Arnold_Kegel Accessed August 15, 2019.

Levry, Joseph Michael. *Naam Yoga Teacher Training Manual*. New York: Rootlight Inc., 2006. Print.

The Sacred Teachings of Kabbalah and Kundalini Yoga: A Vital Course for this Age. Level 1. New York: Rootlight Inc., 1994. Print.

The Sacred Teachings of Kabbalah and Kundalini Yoga: A Vital Course for this Age. Level 2. New York: Rootlight Inc., 1994. Print.

The Sacred Teachings of Kabbalah and Kundalini Yoga: A Vital Course for this Age. Level 3. New York: Rootlight Inc., 1994. Print.

McTaggart, Lynne. *The Field: The Quest for the Secret Force of the Universe.* New York: HarperCollins, 2002. Print.

The Intention Experiment: Using Your Thoughts to Change Your Life and the World. New York: Simon and Schuster, 2007. Print.

Melemi, Steven M. *I Want to Change My Life: How to Overcome Anxiety, Depression and Addiction.* nc: Modern Therapies, 2010. Print.

Miller, Robin H. and Janet Horn. *The Smart Woman's Guide to Midlife and Beyond.* Oakland: New Harbinger Publications, 2008. Print.

Miller, Robin H. and David Es. Kahn. *Healed – Health and Wellness for the 21st Century: Wisdom, Secrets and Fun Straight from the Leading Edge.* Medford: Triune Integrative Medicine, 2017, Print.

Schucman, Helen. *A Course in Miracles: Combined Volume.* Novato, CA: Foundation For Inner Peace, 1975. Print.

Swami Vishnu-devananda. *Shivananda Companion to Yoga.* New York: Fireside Books, 1983. Print.

TheFreeDictionary.com. "FEAR." https://acronyms.thefreedictionary.com/FEA Retrieved August 21, 2019.

Tale of Two Wolves: http://www.nanticokeindians.org/page/tale-of-two-wolves Accessed August 15, 2019.

Unknown Authors. *The Urantia Book*. Chicago: Urantia Foundation, 1984. Print. Wilczek, Frank. *Einstein's Parable of Quantum Insanity*. Published September 10, 2015. https://www.quantamagazine.org/einsteins-parable-of-quantum-insanity-20150910/

Yogananda, Paramahansa. *Autobiography of a Yogi*. Los Angeles: Self-Realization Fellowship, 1974. Print.

Yogi Bhajan. *The Aquarian Teacher: KRI, International Kundalini Yoga Teacher Training, Level One*. First Edition. Santa Cruz: Kundalini Research Institute, Yogi Bhajan, 2003. Print.

Yogi Bhajan and Harbhajan Singh Khalsa. *The Master's Touch*. First Edition. Santa Cruz: Kundalini Research Institute, 1997. Print.

MUSIC:

Clarkson, Kelly. "Miss Independent." Album: *Thankful*. Rhett Lawrence, Producer. Sound Gallery Studios. Los Angeles, 2003. Songwriters: Kelly Clarkson, Rhett Lawrence, Christina Aguilera, Matt Morris. https://youtu.be/dS1ZW0FdoIU

Cook, Jesse. "Beyond Borders." Coach House Music Inc., Canada, 2017. https://www.youtube.com/watch?v=E-r5UFbCYos

"Rumba Foundation." Coach House Music Inc. Distributed by E1 Music, Canada, 2009. https://www.youtube.com/watch?v=OIa_WTcZeFQ

Lennon, John. "Imagine." Phil Spector, John Lennon, and Yoko Ono, Producers. Ascot Sound Studios, New York and Record Plant East, Ascot, 1971. Songwriters: John Lennon and Yoko Ono. https://www.youtube.com/watch?v=VOgFZfRVaww

WORKS CITED LIST

Bolte Taylor, Jill. *My Stroke of Insight: A Brain Scientist's Personal Journey.* London: Plume, 2009. Print.

Braden, Greg. *Resilience from the Heart - The Power to Thrive in Life's Extremes.* Carlsbad: Hay House, 2015. Print.

Branden, Nathaniel. *Six Pillars of Self-Esteem.* New York: Bantam, 1995. Print. Hale, Shannon. *Princess Academy.* New York: Bloomsbury, 2005. Print.

Herzberg, Qin Xue and Larry Herzberg. *Chinese Proverbs and Popular Sayings: With Observations on Culture and Language.* Berkley: Stone Bridge Press, 2012. Print.

Khalsa, Dharma Singh and Cameron Stauth. *Meditation as Medicine: Activate the Power of Your Natural Healing Force.* New York: Fireside, 2002. Print.

McTaggart, Lynn, quoted in Poe, Rahasya. *To Believe or Not to Believe: The Social and Neurological Consequences of Belief Systems.* Bloomington: Xlibris, 2009. Print.

Vonnegut, Kurt. *Deadeye Dick.* New York: Delacorte Press Seymour Lawrence, 1982. Print. Wolf, Fred Alan. *Dr. Quantum's Little Book of Big Ideas: Where Science Meets Spirit.* Newburyport: Red Wheel/Weiser, 2005. Print.

URLS:

Alzheimer's Research and Prevention Foundation. http://alzheimersprevention.org/research/12- minute-memory-exercise/ Published: August 21, 2019

Beck, Aaron T. "Enduring impact on mental health." Harvard Mental Health Letter: https://www.health.harvard.edu/newsletter_article/dr-aaron-t-becks-enduring-impact-on-mental-health Published: October, 2011

Bolte Taylor, Jill. *Ted Talk:* https://www.ted.com/talks/jill_bolte_taylor_s_powerful_stroke_of_insight?language=en

Braden, Gregg, quoted at *Soul Love: Sharing Kindness, Love, and Gratitude:* http://www.soullove.com/2015/11/02/resilience-from-the-heart-gregg-braden/ Accessed September 2016

Braden, Gregg: https://www.hayhouse.com/resilience-from-the-heart-paperback Accessed August 2019

Brooks, Megan. *Frequent Sleeping Pill Use Linked to Increased Dementia Risk.* https://www.medscape.com/viewarticle/915836 Published: July 19, 2019.

Centers for Disease Control and Prevention (CDC) Sleep Study: https://www.cdc.gov/media/releases/2016/p0215-enough-sleep.html Accessed August 2017

Department of Health and Human Services. National Institute for Occupational Safety and Health. "Stress at Work." 1999. Publication No. 99-101: https://www.cdc.gov/niosh/docs/99- 101/ Accessed October 2018

Dictionary.com. https://www.dictionary.com/

Dijk, Derk-Jan. Surrey Sleep Research Centre: https://www.supermemo.com/en/archives1990-2015/articles/sleep Accessed November 2018

Giles, Wayne. "Sleep Review: Taking Sleep Public." CDC's Division of Population Health. August 28, 2014: http://www.sleepreviewmag.com/

Gurmukhī. https://www.merriam-webster.com/dictionary/Gurmukhi Accessed August 2019

Hagelin, John S., Maxwell V. Rainforth, David W. Orme-Johnson, Kenneth L. Cavanaugh, Charles N. Alexander, Susan F. Shatkin, John L. Davies, Anne O. Hughes, and Emanuel Ross. "Effects of Group Practice of the "Transcendental Meditation" Program on Preventing Violent Crime in Washington, D.C.: Results of the National Demonstration Project, June- July 1993." *Social Indicators Research* 47, no. 2 (1999): 153-201: http://www.jstor.org/stable/27522387 Accessed September 2019

Hale, Shannon. https://www.goodreads.com/work/quotes/3299770-princess-academy Accessed November 2018

Harvard Medical Researchers, Sleep Study: http://healthysleep.med.harvard.edu/healthy/matters/consequences/sleep-and-disease-risk Accessed October 2018

Hsieh, Esther. *Tongue Shocks Hasten Healing - Electrically stimulating the tongue may help repair neural damage.* https://www.scientificamerican.com/article/tongue-shocks-hasten- healing/ Published: November 1, 2014. Accessed August 2019

Journal of Clinical Sleep Medicine, Vol. 11, No. 6, April 2015: https://aasm.org/resources/pdf/pressroom/adult-sleep-duration-consensus.pdf Accessed October 2018

James, William. Quotations: BrainyQuote.com, BrainyMedia Inc, 2019: https://www.brainyquote.com/quotes/william_james_104186 Accessed July 20, 2019

Park, Alice. "Alzheimer's Linked to Sleeping Pills and Anti-Anxiety Drugs." *Time Magazine*. September 10, 2014:

https://time.com/3313927/alzheimers-linked-to-sleeping-pills-and-anti-anxiety-drugs/ Accessed January 2019

Systems Neurobiology Laboratory, Department of Neurobiology, David Geffen School of Medicine, University of California. Los Angeles, CA. 90095. USA. Accessed September 2018

RESOURCES

To access supplemental materials for your Do-Be-Do-Be-Do-Be lifestyle, please visit:
www.DoDoRescue.com

To find out more about Louise's live classes and programs, visit:
www.joyfull-yoga.com

To access the full list of online programs currently available with Louise, visit:
www.Foundation4yourLIFE.com

To find out more about Louise, visit:
www.LouiseLavergne.com

To buy massage rings and more eco-friendly and fair trade items, you can visit Louise's partner store:
www.picosworldwide.com

NOTES

NOTES

NOTES

NOTES

NOTES

NOTES

NOTES

NOTES

NOTES

NOTES

NOTES

www.ingramcontent.com/pod-product-compliance
Lightning Source LLC
Chambersburg PA
CBHW052054110526
44591CB00013B/2207